**The Apophis Club Draconian Magic Series**

*APOPHIS*
*Ægishjálmur: The Book of Dragon Runes*
*Dragonscales*
*Draconian Consciousness*
*Words of Power*
*The Grimoire of the Sevenfold Serpent*
*Gods and Monsters*
*Runes of Mann*
*The Sevenfold Mystery*
*Everything and Nothing*
*The Satanic Dragon* (forthcoming)
*The Draconian Quadrilogy* (the first four books above in a single, large format volume)

**The Apophis Club Practical Guide Series**

*How To Read Ogham*
*How To Conjure a Spirit*
*How To Astral Travel*
*How To Make and Use Talismans*
*How To Read Tarot*
*How To Do Sex Magic*
*How To Be a Necromancer* (forthcoming)

**The Apophis Club Lesser Magic Series**

*The Masks of Lesser Magic* (forthcoming)

**www.theapophisclub.com**

https://www.facebook.com/TheApophisClub

# EVERYTHING & NOTHING

by Michael Kelly

*A Publication of The Apophis Club*

*Dedicated to the memory of*

***David Austen***

*a great friend and a Great Noble,*

*a Master of Magic*

# Table of Contents

# PREFACE

It's probably as well for me to explain this book before you read it. Because it's likely to offend and upset a lot of people. And by 'a lot of people', I don't mean the general public, I mean magicians – even members of The Apophis Club!

You see, in these pages, I deliberately attack a lot of cherished beliefs. And I don't mean religious beliefs, I mean notions and opinions held by magicians that I feel are either false or which actually have no evidence to support them. This is likely to get a lot of people's hackles up.

Indeed, in the first, *solve*, part of the book, it may appear to some that I have turned my back on magic and the occult altogether. This is not the truth at all, which is why I am asking you here **in advance** to bear with me. In the *coagula* section you will see me gradually rebuild a coherent magical model after first levelling the ruins of the old world, and the closing, *everything and nothing*, section has many passages of soaring magical beauty. So stick with it, you may be amazed and heartened by what results.

But first you will need to join me in tearing down the painted scenery and slaughtering the sacred cows in *solve*. And it will be painful. But if a belief cannot stand up to challenge, it is false, and the magician is a seeker after Truth.

Illusion may be our trade, but it is not our Vision.

You may, of course, disagree with some of what I write. This is your prerogative. I am trying to encourage questioning, not enforce dogma. I am a challenger, not a debunker. Nevertheless, it should be understood that after three decades' experience of magic, during two of which I have rubbed shoulders with the very highest of my peers, this book represents a true evaluation of magic as I currently see it. I believe the 'Runes For Sceptics' chapter to be one of the most profound and philosophically beautiful I have ever written, especially when expanded with the material from the third, *everything and nothing*, section of the book.

This challenging, radical book is actually a gift. Far from being a debunk, it actually asserts that yes, magic really works, and it offers a profound magical worldview in its conclusions. But it does not tolerate superstition or unratified belief. The magic presented here is far more reliable, powerful and transformational than any approach I have otherwise found. It has taken me decades to streamline and fine tune this model and I wish to save you time by learning from my own painful lessons.

You need not agree with all of my conclusions, but that is not the point. Your beliefs should be open to challenge and investigation. After that, your conclusions are your own.

Finally, read this book **very** carefully. Some parts are deliberately worded with a view to pressing readers' hot buttons in order to challenge their thinking. Do **not** skim read. Sometimes a single word, easily glossed over, changes the whole tenor of a sentence. But this book was not written for popularity, but as a genuine expression of tough love, to raise up smarter and far more powerful magicians. It is in this spirit that these words are offered.

- Michael Kelly, 11 May 2016

# WHAT'S IT ALL ABOUT?

Previous volumes in The Apophis Club's Draconian Magic series have basically been practical instruction manuals, with the occasional collection of essays and articles to illuminate or elaborate upon certain specific areas. This new volume, entitled *Everything and Nothing*, is quite different in both structure and purpose.

This is primarily a volume of philosophy rather than practice. It is a volume that is now sorely needed, as the occult in general – including the Left-Hand Path – becomes increasingly mired in superstition, loose thinking, unfounded beliefs and old habits which are taking far too long to die. Draconian Magic Works upon the Real, and without a clear and precise Understanding of what is Real, you cannot hope to master it.

The book is divided into three sections and it should be read in this precise order. When a new recruit begins military training, they are first subjected to experiences and rigours which break down the person they were before enlisting, leaving them a relatively blank slate. Only then can they be rebuilt through discipline and training into a well-drilled fighting machine. The same is true for magicians, or at least for those who aspire to Mastery.

Therefore, the first two sections of the book follow the old alchemical process of *solve et coagula*: in the first section, magic is deconstructed and taken to pieces, discarding all the flim-flam until its purest Essence is revealed and unsullied; only then can it be rebuilt into a coherent and powerful engine in the second section. The third section employs this new Understanding of magic to address some of the most common questions people pose about life, the universe and everything.

The *solve* section of the book will undoubtedly prove to be the most controversial thing I have ever written. I will be slaughtering a whole herd of sacred cows, debunking superstitions and challenging loose thinking. Every magical school tries to Awaken its Initiates and break the chains of conditioning and convention which bind them; however, very few challenge some of the worst chains of the lot: the errors and general rubbish which constitutes 90%+ of occultism itself. There will be some very cherished and widely held beliefs dragged screaming into the light of day where they will evaporate into nothing in this section, and there will be very few – if any – readers who do not feel their hackles rise as some cherished belief or practice is thrown to the dogs. I make no apologies for this, as I am more concerned with making strong and empowered Initiates than providing comfortable half-truths. If you do not want your illusions to be shattered – if you do not want to become truly Initiate instead of just an occultist – do not read this book.

After demolishing superstition and plain wrong thinking, the second *coagula* section will look at the pure kernel of magic that remains and create a fresh Reality from it, allowing a true knowledge and understanding of magic and the Real to develop and grow, informing the Initiate's Work and leading to profound insights and unprecedented magical success.

Finally, this new insight is applied to the great philosophical questions which people are always asking: why are we here? how did the universe begin? what is the meaning of life? why is there evil in the world? For there are clear and satisfactory answers – or at least, approaches to answers – to all of these questions once the bullshit has been cleared away. And they're **not** the usual garbage that you've heard a thousand times before. If, like me, you've ground your teeth upon hearing "everything happens for a purpose" one time too often, you'll love this section. But in order to properly appreciate it, you'll have to work through the *solve et coagula* process first.

The title of this book, *Everything and Nothing*, has a multitude of meanings. You will find that some of these feel more appropriate the more you read the book and come to Understand it. First time round, as you're sore because I've rubbished some of the things you may have held sacred, you may feel that the book promised Everything and gave you Nothing; later, as its perspective starts to paint a new picture of Reality, you may feel that it reduced your prior worldview to Nothing, but provided Everything in return; as Understanding and Mastery dawn, you will discover that Everything and Nothing are Truth in the most sublime sense.

This, I guess, is my *Book of Lies*, and it comes complete with all the challenges and paradoxes and heresies of that volume. Read it and weep...

# SOLVE

# The Hogwash School of Witchcraft and Wizardry

"Seek After the Mysteries", the English meaning of Magus Stephen Edred Flowers' formula *Reyn til Runa*, is the clarion call of every genuine school of magic (or something very much like it, if not these exact words). But something very tragic befalls almost every such seeker. Even as we strive to discover and illuminate the genuine Mysteries of life, we tend instead to become more and more entangled in the mysterious, wrapped around in obscuring fogs of mystical obscurantism, half truths, assumed knowledge, unquestioned 'facts', all mired in acres of good, old-fashioned bullshit.

And believe me when I say that I'm not simply wagging a stern finger at other people here. I know this because I've been there. Everything I have learned and Become has been at the cost of hard graft, harder lessons and often painful experience.

The occult world is full of comforting lies, told by well-meaning people, and this bumfluff is accepted by those who have struggled and managed to win their freedom from the lies that society has told them and which have been imposed upon them by the media and politicians every day of their lives. It is a terrible and shameful fact that these new magicians, people who have torn themselves free from conformity and convention, just as Set the Mighty tore Himself free from the womb of the Cosmos, should then be trapped in new bonds forged by the very schools they hoped would teach them freedom. But so much of what passes for 'genuine' magical lore is a shallow sham, accepted on the rebound, instead of a genuine love affair.

Everyone who becomes a magician experiences this to some degree. Even those of us lucky enough to have received our training in schools where Truth was paramount and where Teachers could be found who told us exactly how things were, would still be lulled into a soporific slumber occasionally, so all-pervasive is the curse of occultism.

So there are no mocking fingers being pointed here, we have all been there and we can all slip back so easily. But here, if you will have it, is the Hogwash School of Witchcraft and Wizardry. Here, your most fondly held illusions will be dispelled, your superstitions will be flayed from you, the very foundations of your belief will be smashed beneath your feet, until you stand in a Void, stripped of all. Then, the Work of Remanifestation can begin and you can learn Real Magic in Truth.

But first comes the hard and painful part. So let's start naming and shaming that bullshit and shredding that loose thinking...

# THE THREE TYPES OF MAGIC AND HOW THEY WORK

To begin with, it will be helpful for us to define the different types of magic. This will help us more clearly to identify the processes involved. Now I'm not talking about those old chestnuts 'Black Magic and White Magic' here, although there is an interesting philosophical distinction between the two. For now, I'm thinking of far more pragmatic and process-oriented definitions: methods rather than motives, if you will.

In the Temple of Set, the magical school in which I earned my Mastery[1], magic was initially divided into two broad categories. These were Greater Magic, which was concerned with the transformation and magical development of the Self, and Lesser Magic, which was the use of psychological and other skills to manipulate others and your circumstances in order to effect the results you desired.

Greater Magic was generally practised in the setting of a ritual chamber (or outdoors), using ceremonial techniques. It used ritual, artistic symbolism and invocation amongst other techniques to enter a state of consciousness in which the psyche could apprehend truths and insights which it

1 See *The Confessions of Michael Kelly, Vol. 3: The Children of Set* for full details.

could then use to fashion its future becoming. These insights could be used to enhance life, transform the Self, and steer your course in the direction you wished your life to take.

Lesser Magic used techniques such as suggestion, misdirection, body language, stage magic techniques and general bamboozlement to persuade, influence and direct other persons and organisations in such a way as to promote your own agenda, enabling you to achieve what you wanted.

When I joined the Temple, these were the two distinctions made in magical practice. During my sojourn, a third category was added: that which became known as Medial Magic. Medial Magic was basically 'results' magic – aimed at the acquisition of everyday things, such as love, money, revenge, etc., the kinds of things which would otherwise be the province of Lesser Magic – using ritual methods. In other words, it was Lesser Magical goals targeted by Greater Magical techniques.

Now, before we proceed any further it is necessary to address the elephant in the room and ask, purely and plainly: does magic work? Because if it doesn't, we may as well all close this book and go about our business. But yes, thankfully it does. After thirty years' applied magical practice, I can honestly tell you that magic works. And the more you practice it, the more skilled you become, and the better it works. Magic can accomplish the seemingly impossible.

Having said that, I am going to make the first of many statements in this *solve* section which will initially seem absolutely outrageous and will have most practising magicians reading this spitting feathers. Are you ready? Here it comes:

**Almost all successful magic involves no supernatural element whatsoever.**

Have you got that? Have you finished choking and spluttering in indignation yet? Okay, let me explain why this is so by returning to our three varieties of magic and explaining the successful operation of each in turn.

I guess we should begin with Lesser Magic, since the statement is quite easy to comprehend with respect to this. Lesser Magic works by utilising skills with psychological techniques in order to get what you want. There are several different levels of Lesser Magic, but all of them utilise perfectly natural phenomena. The magician may beguile with wit and charm, using charisma and confidence to win over his target; he may employ sleight of hand or other modes of trickery to effect a result; he may utilise hypnotic language, embedded suggestions and similar techniques of programming a response on a subconscious level. He may cast a glamour through dress and appearance, bewitching with colour and music and mood. But in all cases, he is using his own wits and skills to form an impression in the psyche of his target which will lead that target to give him what he wants. His methods will be tailored to the situation, whether trying to seduce someone, negotiate a business deal, successfully pass a job interview, or whatever. If he is skilled enough and has learned the tricks of Lesser Magic, his sorcery will be successful, but at no point will he have used any supernatural agency, although it may sometimes seem as though he **must** have done to witnesses who see him pull off some unlikely coup. This is the magic of Derren Brown, of Jedi mind tricks, of Svengali. And it is by far the best type of magic to use if you want to get things done your way, though beginners tend to shy away from it because it takes a lot of practice to learn and a lot of skill to develop. You inevitably fall flat on your face and bloody your nose more than a few times while learning the ropes. Hardly any magical schools teach these techniques. The Temple of Set and the Church of Satan certainly give attention to Lesser Magic but personal, one on one training is a rarity. This is something I plan to remedy within The Apophis Club.

Greater Magic is quite different. The most important magical Work is Work upon the Self. This is what Initiation is all about, the transformation from a man in the street into someone who has become more conscious, more Awake, more aware of the world around them and the potential of both themselves and the world. Someone who is determined to become something greater than they previously were. This kind of magic is worked through ritual methods. The magician may manipulate a symbol set, such as runes, to define what he is seeking, or may call upon spirits or divine figures. But what does this ritual process do? Are we really to believe that the lighting of candles, the utterance of scripted conjurations, the movements and the symbols can actually have any true power over reality?

Actually, they do. Not directly upon the nuts and bolts of the Cosmos, perhaps, but the ritual procedure has a fascinating and focusing effect upon the magician's own mind. By entering into this sequence of unusual, ritualised events and recitals, quite distinct and separate from the daily routine of workaday life, the psyche is put in a strange and receptive mode, a form of self-hypnosis. In this condition, the usual gulfs which divide the conscious and subconscious minds are – at least to some degree, depending upon the skill of the magician – bridged, and the whole mind may be accessed and put to use. The subconscious takes in **everything**, much of which is filtered out of conscious awareness. These filters are created by habit, conditioning, cultural expectations, personal belief systems, and many other factors. But the ritual lowers them, at least partially, for a time, by hypnotically leading the expectant mind into a place where it can be afforded a glimpse into its own depths. The magician's perception and understanding then become so much more complete than they were, solutions may be seen to problems, bad habits may be erased, creativity may be ignited; in short, the magician may emerge from the ritual **changed** on some inner level which can then be channelled through to adjust his life and circumstances in a permanent way.

This is **not** the result of the ritual. It is the result of the magician's self-induced suggestibility which leads to a greater cohesion of mind, giving access to resources and insights which are usually obscured and hidden away. Having experienced this process a few times, a genuine Adept no longer needs ritual to recreate this state of mind; he can recall it at need.

So, the magical changes and transformations in the magician's life are actually brought into being by the perfectly natural process of focusing his own mind upon a question. He has simply learned the skill of doing so to an extent which non-magicians tend not to be familiar with (though artists and writers do tend to be able to access a similar state of mind in their creative works).

Looking at a good example, I recall that the Temple of Set's encyclopaedic volume for Adepts, *The Ruby Tablet of Set*, used to contain a ritual script titled 'The Fat Lady Ritual'. This had been penned by an Initiate who was unhappy about her size and wrote a ritual to help her lose weight. So how would this ritual work? Would it zap away a few pounds of flab in a blinding flash? No, obviously not. It directed her focus, opened her mind, and allowed her to access and reprogram her subconscious so that she would eat less and healthier, and exercise more. Note that this is a completely different thing than simply boosting her willpower to diet; it involves an **actual change in her personality matrix** on a deep level, so that bad habits are adjusted and new patterns of behaviour and attitude introduced. This is much, much more than mere 'positive thinking' or willpower; this magician has actually effected a transformation within herself. But the important thing to note is that **nothing** supernatural has occurred. She has used the mind that she has in order to effect the change. The nature of this change and the skill to bring it about are certainly not things that anybody can accomplish without magical training, the degree of Self-control and Self-knowledge evidenced are far beyond the scope of the ordinary man in the street. But it is by no means supernatural.

Now there are other applications of Greater Magic, in which the magician may become oracular, supposedly connecting with the consciousness of a God or spirit, or may journey in the mind to other-dimensional realities. Such types of magical Working are too big in their scope to be examined under this umbrella heading, so will be addressed in detail later in this *solve* section. For now, it is sufficient to have examined the process of Greater Magical ritual and the transformations which may be effected within the Self, recognising that at this basic level there is no requirement for any supernatural explanation: the process is highly skilled and difficult to do, but it is a function of the human mind.

So what about Medial Magic, the use of ritual methods to create change in others, or in the environment, instead of in yourself? Oh, this is where it really gets cunning!

With Medial Magic, we are talking about such magical operations as attracting money, or love, or a new job, or perhaps cursing an enemy. And we are seeking to achieve these things through ritual techniques. Does Medial Magic actually work and deliver the desired results? Yes, it does. So how can I possibly extend my absurd assertion that most successful magic involves no supernatural element to this kind of ritual results magic?

The first step in answering this question (because yes, my rule most definitely still applies) is to consider firstly the nature of the ritual and the effect that it has upon the psyche of the magician. The ritual will be devised with the purpose of focusing the Will exclusively upon the goal. There will be pertinent colours and symbols used. Appropriate names of power may be called upon. Sigils and talismans may be created. Demons may be evoked. All will be appropriate to the purpose of the rite. Exactly as with Greater Magic, this has the effect of turning the magician's mind inwards, focusing it upon the matter in question, and increasing the flow-through of information between the conscious and subconscious through the auto-suggestion created by the ritual. The effect that this interchange has upon the overall consciousness of the magician has two aspects, one passive and one active. Passively, it adjusts the magician's perspective upon the matter, making him feel more confident in relation to the goal, viewing it as something which must now inevitably come to pass, virtually a *fait accompli*. This has the inevitable knock-on effect of making the magician behave differently with regard to the matter, since he believes it is already decided in his favour. This more confident and positive approach can in itself sometimes be all that is required to swing the balance. Actively, the spell works upon the most malleable substance available to it – the magician's own mind – to carry out its function. So if the magician has cast a love spell, the reason being that his crippling shyness has never permitted him to ask out the girl of his dreams, he suddenly finds himself with the courage and resolve to do precisely that; moreover, the newfound confidence the magic has engendered within him will boost his charisma and make him much more likely to receive a positive response. If he has conjured for money, he is suddenly able to recall an item stored in the attic which he can sell on ebay for more than enough to cover his immediate need; or he is impelled to apply for a new, more lucrative job opportunity which he would previously not have noticed or would have been too lazy to consider. In all cases, the magician becomes far more aware of opportunities and actions which are always there, but which are usually ignored or suppressed. What the magic does is make him far more aware and alert to the possibilities which exist to bring about his desired goal; it does not create these possibilities, it points them out and makes them obvious. And it certainly doesn't do the work for him; he still has to make the decisive move which fulfils the spell.

What is apparent in nearly all cases is that the Medial Magic ritual does not alter the surrounding reality directly. Instead, it acts upon the consciousness of the magician, enabling him to see the already existing paths to success, and boosting his confidence and abilities to the extent that he is able to carry out those necessary tasks successfully. An honest appraisal of successful magical Workings – three decades' experience of them in my own case – will reveal this to be true in almost all cases. So once again, we are able to see that my little law holds true in the case of Medial Magic, with most successes requiring no supernatural element at all.

Of course, the rubric and thrust of most Medial Magic rituals are geared so that it **seems** as if the ritual itself is the engine which will effect the result. This is because magicians – especially in their early careers – like to bolster themselves with these crutches, still uncertain of the real power of the unified mind. We can therefore see that, amusingly, Medial Magic can actually be defined as the trappings of Greater Magic being used as a technique of Lesser Magic to fool our own selves into going out and achieving the changes we want the magic to accomplish.

You may be going into full-on defensive mode by now and insisting that there are many results achieved through magic which cannot be explained in this way. Maybe there are, but remember my rule states that **almost all** have no supernatural element. Perhaps the few who don't quite fit that 'almost' do? We'll deal with that in the *coagula* section, but before we can even think about the supernatural, we need a clear appreciation of what actually happens in a successful Working of magic. This current chapter dealing with the three types of magic has furnished us with two verifiable facts: magic of all three types does indeed bring the results it claims to; it works. But in nearly all cases, it is clear that no supernatural element is required in order to explain that success. Later, after reading sections two and three of the book, you may choose to decide that (according to your belief) these operations do incorporate a factor which is transcendental and outside the normal laws of physics. Or you may not. But neither position will alter the simple truth I have revealed here of how magic actually works; it does not **require** such a supernatural factor. I know several atheists and materialists who regularly achieve magical results far more quickly and spectacularly than those who believe firmly in spirits and astral planes. This doesn't prove either of them to be correct, but it does demonstrate the absolute neutrality of magic on the issue.

There will be several people holding up a finger to remonstrate at this point and going, "Ah, but..." Don't! Because having looked at these three broad categories, we're now going to go on to slaughter a whole herd of sacred cows as I start to look at specifics. You may be surprised. But in any case, before we start to rebuild in the *coagula* section, we are going to dismantle the whole magical edifice piece by piece.

## DIVINATION

Let's start by taking a close look at the divinatory arts, one of the most popular and most passive of magical skills, also one which most practitioners insist requires the greatest degree of spiritual perception and intuitive openness. This incorporates such practices as reading Tarot, runes or ogham, interpreting astrological charts, or the more free-form techniques of prophecy.

If we look at Tarot to begin with, as the comments we make about Tarot can be equally applied to similar divinatory practices using runes or ogham, in which symbolic tokens are placed in positions of specific meaning by a random process.

The Tarot deck consists of two types of card: the twenty two symbolic picture cards of the Major Arcana, and the fifty six number and court cards of the Minor Arcana. In more recent times, commencing with the French occultists of the Nineteenth Century and most popularised in the writings of Eliphas Levi, and leading through to the Hermetic Order of the Golden Dawn, who refined the system, the Tarot has been attributed to and combined with the symbolic models of the Qabalah. The twenty two Major Arcana cards are attributed to the letters of the Hebrew alphabet and thus ultimately to the twenty two paths of the diagram of the Tree of Life. The numbered cards 1 through 10 of each suit of the Minor Arcana are attributed to the ten Sephiroth; the four court cards of each suit, and the suits themselves, are attributed to the four Qabalistic world levels and to the four classical Elements. Furthermore, each Sephirah and each Path has its own Elemental, Planetary or zodiacal attribution, which is carried over to the card(s) related to it. So the Tarot becomes a symbolic picture book of the entirety of Qabalistic magical philosophy.

Both Qabalah and Tarot have been utilised in different ways by magicians for centuries, and even the more recent Golden Dawn model has now seen extensive use and adjustment and philosophical speculation for well over a century. As such, it has been balanced and counter-balanced until it is a precise and accurate portrayal of all aspects of human psychological experience. This is true whether you interpret the symbols of the Tarot as eternal spiritual principles or as aspects of the human psyche; the Tarot is a balanced, complex and comprehensive psychological map whether you are a spiritualist or a materialist, it simply is what it is.

So anybody who has studied magic which inherits elements from the Golden Dawn (as most occult books and systems do) will find themselves very comfortable with the symbolism of the Tarot, finding the cards and their associations very meaningful.

In divination, the cards are shuffled, randomising their order, then they are laid out according to a predetermined pattern, with a view to providing insight into a question which the querent has posed to the Tarot reader. The positions in the pattern of the layout (or the 'spread') have meanings of their own, which are then referenced against the meaning of the card that is dealt there. Finally, all of the meanings of all of the cards and their positions are balanced against each other to tell an often detailed story which ultimately leads to a solution or insight relating to the question.

The first question that we need to ask is: does a Tarot reading work? Can a reader lay out the cards and gain fresh and pertinent insight which will be of real practical help to his querent? After thirty years' experience of Tarot reading, I can unequivocally say yes, it does work, once the reader has gained the required experience. I often give startlingly accurate readings which give querents much food for thought and have been responsible for major changes and improvements in peoples' lives.

There are all manner of theories which try to explain how divination works. Some will tell you that a skilled diviner taps into other levels of reality, channelling spiritual forces which guide the shuffler's hands to ensure that the right cards fall in the right places. Others will tell you that fate or destiny is set in stone and that someone who is trained in Tarot reading cannot fail to lay out the correct, predestined cards. Some will insist that incorporeal spirits literally influence the shuffle. Others will suggest that a Tarot reader who is familiar with the cards and their meanings is sensitive to their vibrations and will be 'guided' to lay the correct cards in the correct places. Carl Jung suggested, as part of his theory of synchronicity, that each moment in time has a kind of signature and that the cards placed at the time a question is asked will have a definite resonance with the subject of the question at that time, allowing the reading to afford genuine insight. Others will tell you it's all pure bunkum, but since we have already established the accuracy of a Tarot reading from an experienced hand (by which I mean a magician, trained over long years, not a fairground 'psychic'), there must be a little more to it than that.

One thing that most of these theories have in common, however, and which is fully borne out by experience, is that contrary to fairground fortune-teller expectations, the Tarot cards do **not** foretell the future. That is not the purpose of divination, which is to gain clear insight into a situation so that the right choices may be made in order to fashion the kind of future that we want. Divination is a magical means of reading the patterns of events in the present. Now inevitably, if we are able to discern the patterns manifesting in present situations, we may be able to discern the ways in which those patterns will continue and unfold, thus gaining an insight into **probable** or **possible** futures, which may change depending upon how we interact with those patterns now. But such is reasoned extrapolation, not a fated future.

So, does my non-supernatural rule hold true with a Tarot reading? Yes, it does: almost all Tarot readings involve no supernatural elements whatsoever. In fact, in the case of divination, you might even omit the word 'almost' and just say '**all**'.

So what is actually the mechanism which decides which card is placed in which position after shuffling in a Tarot reading? This is perfectly easy to answer: the mechanism in question is pure random chance[2]. The shuffling of the cards very effectively randomises their order and there is no preference or significance in which card ultimately lands in which stead of meaning in the spread; it could equally well be any of them. There is no agency at all to ensure that the 'right' cards land in the 'right' places; it simply does not happen.

So, if the placing of the cards is not and cannot be in itself significant, but divination nevertheless furnishes genuine insights and good advice, how can this possibly be the case?

---

2 There is one very important exception to this, relating to stage magic when a card may be 'forced'; it doesn't concern us here when looking at 'vanilla' divination.

What is it that in fact happens? The simple fact is that when a proper reader – a skilled magician – reads the Tarot, he will do so in a similar manner to the way in which he approaches any other magical Working. His attention and Will become focused upon the matter in question and a trance-like state is entered, during which the conscious and subconscious are able to exchange and communicate much more coherently and readily. The meanings of the cards and the steads in which they are placed already hold considerable symbolic significance to a practised reader. These meanings will coalesce within his mind, merging with his current understanding of the situation, and **enhanced by the deeper, subconscious recognition of underlying patterns of which he now becomes aware, but which ordinarily lie below the threshold of awareness.** It is the intuitive apprehension of these subconsciously perceived underlying traits – which he already knew but was not previously consciously aware of – that are the foremost factor in enabling the Tarot reader to deliver a devastatingly accurate reading. This is *assisted* by the cards chosen, because even though they are a completely random selection, each of them will suggest some new way of looking at the situation, providing the querent with alternative perspectives and suggestions that they have probably never considered, in a kind of symbolic 'brainstorming' session. These two factors taken together provide a very powerful and effective analysis of the situation, coupled with a range of creative suggestions and potential solutions. A skilled reading such as this may not be supernatural as commonly understood, but its value is pure gold.

Exactly the same process is true when other tools such as runestaves or ogham fews are used for divination. Like the Tarot, each rune or ogham is a packed symbolic entity, and when placed or cast and interpreted in relation to each other, these – combined with the reader's subconscious uprising of operant patterns – will inform an accurate and insightful reading.

On the surface of it, astrology may appear to be a completely different thing, since its factors are not random, but depend upon the calculation of fixed positions of astronomical bodies and their relative positioning at a given point in time. But in point of fact, the actual divinatory process is exactly the same. The stars and their positions influence nothing, they have not the slightest discernible effect upon our affairs. Instead, the discipline and concentration involved in preparing the chart and calculating the aspects perform the familiar effect of drawing together the reader's conscious and subconscious, focused upon the querent's situation. Then the **mythic** qualities attributed to the Planets and Signs and Houses all combine in the reader's mind to accomplish the same function as Tarot cards, runes or ogham, suggesting new ways of viewing or approaching a situation, pointing out suggestions never previously considered.

This is why it requires a skilled reader, with many years of practice, to give a worthwhile reading. Because it is the meaning of the symbols, brought alive through long study and understanding in the reader's mind, coupled with the ability to bridge the conscious / subconscious divide, that furnishes the reading. A beginner without such discipline and training is simply laying out random pictures printed on card, with no rhyme nor reason; these things have no intrinsic power in themselves, only in the prepared and trained mind. And then, as can be seen, the procedure – whilst remarkable, uncanny and spellbinding, potentially life-changing – is not a supernatural matter.

# ASTRAL TRAVEL

Another mainstay of modern magicians is the phenomenon generally termed astral travel (also known as 'travelling in the spirit vision', 'vision quests', 'shamanic journeying', etc.). This is a practice whereby the magician allows his body to relax and enter an immobile, almost catatonic state, whilst his consciousness leaves its usual moorings and goes off exploring other dimensions, other planes of existence.

Very rarely will astral travel be an unfocused or vague process. The magician has generally prepared for the experience in advance through invoking specific Elemental, Planetary, Qabalistic, Enochian, runic or other powers, focusing his Will upon the precise region of the Magical Universe he wishes to visit. He will also generally have some visual representation of the desired region before him as a focus for Will. This may be a sigil, a rune, a Tarot image, or anything else which is pertinent to the purpose of his journey.

When the ritual preparations are complete, the magician relaxes completely, closes his eyes and focuses upon a visualised representation of his wish. Again, this may be an intense visualisation of a sigil, a rune, a Planetary Seal or whatnot. Sometimes a landscape will then gradually appear before his inner vision; other times, he may visualise the sigil upon a door and mentally imagine himself stepping through that door and finding himself in the landscape beyond. In either case, he may then explore this landscape and find there the insights he is seeking.

In a variant to this practice, termed skrying, the magician will instead quiet his body and then stare into a reflective surface, such as a mirror, a pool of ink, or the traditional crystal ball. In skrying, he witnesses visions passing within or upon the surface which holds his eyes rather than actually entering into the visionary experience.

There are three main theories about what actually happens when a magician undertakes an astral journey, and these are recounted below.

The first theory is that the other planes and dimensions of the Magical Universe are objectively real. In this worldview, the magician's consciousness literally leaves his body and travels to another plane of existence. He is able to accomplish this because alongside our physical body, we all also possess a series of subtle bodies, each one appropriate for use upon its own subtle plane. When astral travelling, the magician's consciousness transitions into a subtle body, in which he can move around and interact with the plane he is visiting.

The second theory also holds that the other planes are objectively real places, located in dimensions beyond the physical. But this theory holds that the magician doesn't actually 'travel' anywhere. Instead, the imagination functions as an interface, building an imaginary but accurate representation of the desired plane, in which the magician can move and interact in an imagined body. This theory interprets astral travel as something similar to daydreaming (or indeed, deep night dreaming if the magician's trance state is sufficient), but one which is directed by Will and making a genuine connection with other-planar reality, through which real insights and knowledge may come.

It is worth noting that some psychologists make use of similar techniques in therapy sessions, helping their patients to visualise themselves in new, peaceful locations, then hypnotically (or otherwise) guiding them to explore these locations to obtain insights into their problems. The final theory postulates that the astral realms are no different to the psychologists' methods: the magician creates an environment within his own psyche which reflects his purpose and then seeks answers and wisdom relating to that purpose by exploring the environment in which he finds itself. But according to this theory, the entire experience takes place within the magician's own mind and has no objective existence outside those confines. This does not invalidate the method, as this symbolic exploration of a magical principle, shaped and guided by the subconscious, can give access to huge reservoirs of information and insight; it's simply that it all occurs within the magician's own skull. Any entities met and communicated with in the visited realm are thus interpreted as dream manifestations from the deep places of the magician's own subconscious (and very important, to be heeded, for that precise reason).

To make an informed judgement on this question, we should consider what precisely the magical planes are deemed to be and how they are arranged.

They are arranged according to the cosmology of the tradition in question. But the first stumbling block we encounter is that although some of them are similar, not all of these cosmologies are the same, and some are quite contradictory. For example, although nearly every tradition views the Magical Universe as a gigantic tree, there is heated debate concerning the placing of the physical, material world (and by world we mean the entire physical Cosmos) in this model. Most of the European and shamanic traditions place our physical realm at the centre of the tree. The trunk and branches lead into Divine realms high above, fanning out to touch the primal creative forces, whilst other pathways lead down to the Underworld, from which the nourishment and life force of the Universe arises. But other traditions, such as the Qabalah, or the Enochian system, see the material world as the last and least exalted manifestation of Creation; it is appended to the very bottom of the Qabalistic Tree of Life, and is similarly beneath the Æthyrs which rise from it up into the infinite regions in the Enochian cosmology.

These differences are not irreconcilable if we consider that the cosmological models are representative of principles and creative forces, not literal place maps. But in making this adjustment, we necessarily bring into question the objective existence of these planes, at least in a fixed and dogmatic format.

The Qabalistic Tree of Life consists of ten Sephiroth, linked by twenty two paths which run between them, linking them. These Sephiroth represent emanations of Divine force, descending from a monad down into the variety of the material world.

The Norse World Tree, Yggdrasil, has the material world at its centre (Midgard = 'middle enclosure'). Midgard is surrounded by worlds defined by primal creative forces (fire and ice, verdancy and stability), with higher worlds leading to the realms of the Light Elves and Asgard, where the Gods sit, and down to the underworld of the Dwarfs and ultimately to the domain of Hel. Paths attributed to the runes run between the worlds (Bifrost, the Rainbow Bridge).

The Celtic (Irish) cosmic map is similar to the Norse, with our physical world in the centremost point of reality, with a vast Otherworld symbolically above and an Underworld below, a network of plains and lands joined by paths signified by the ogham.

All of these models do share a common purpose, which they each fulfil extremely well: they balance and counter-balance all of the cosmic, mythic forces in that tradition's conception of the Cosmos, as well as the mythic forces which shape and have dominion in the human psyche. The fact that they are all effective and comprehensive suggests that they each incorporate the same, or similar, forces and symbolic regions. This speaks volumes for the authenticity and usefulness of these models in psychological terms. But although they each contain similar themes and ideas, and although some are certainly more closely akin than others, and although it is possible to deconstruct them all, rearranging and revising their parts to compare with each other, in no case is it possible to simply superimpose one magical tradition's map upon another's. This would tend to rule out the first, most literal, theory of astral travel, which would require a single model to be correct and absolute, not a shifting arrangement in which the territory can adjust to fit the map. But it would not necessarily negate the feasibility of the second theory, in which the imagination acts as a mirror in which the qualities of the desired realm are projected and experienced by the magician. In this case, the invoked realm is real and the imagination is used as an interface between it and the magician's consciousness. The magician's traditional cosmic map is then used as a personal guide to access a given state of being / cosmic quality, it need not be a literal plan of fixed landmarks, only a mental trajectory.

So it can be reasonably established that an astral journey is something that takes place in the imagination of the magician, guided and directed by the magical Will. It remains to decide whether the experience is solely an imaginative construct, or whether it is some kind of reflection of, or interchange with, a 'real astral location'. This can best be decided after considering the next chapter.

## Of Matter and Spirit

Most occult traditions assert matter and spirit are two distinct things. In the Qabalah, the Tree of Life represents a series of emanations which roll outwards from the Divine creative source, becoming progressively denser and more specialised until they ultimately become manifest in matter in Malkuth, a tenth Sephirah which hangs suspended beneath the Tree.

The assertion is that the Sephiroth above Malkuth are somehow distinct from it, made of more subtle spiritual substance, which is malleable and can be reshaped and directed. This quality is used to explain the multi-faceted nature of the astral plane. It is often asserted that on an astral, spiritual level, "thoughts are things". We will come back to this.

A similar kind of dualistic model was employed within the Temple of Set, where I earned my magical laurels. It was felt that there was a clear distinction between the world of things, the universe outside of your skull, and your own thoughts and inner imaginings. There was an objective universe, governed by the laws of physics, and there was an inner, subjective universe, which was yours alone.

These dualistic models are highly effective ones for magicians to employ in their magic: they explain how a magical Working effects a change in the subjective universe; this change is then mirrored to a greater or lesser degree in the objective universe, the extent of the outer change depending upon the passion and precision of the magician. The one thing this model has never been able to manage is to identify the means by which the one influences the other, either falling back on undefined and ultimately meaningless labels such as 'the Magical Link', or else mumbling about things such as 'resonance', but never getting around to explaining how something with no material substance can resonate with something composed of 'real world stuff'.

Thus, the model falls far short and explains nothing; it simply provides an impassable philosophical gulf. It remains a very clever and useful model for assisting novice magicians in developing their rituals and measuring their success. But a model is all that it is, a 'lie for children'.

Some Eastern philosophies deny this dualistic thinking and assert that everything is spirit and that the material world is mere illusion. But even in doing this, they create a distinction and a new duality to replace the old one. By denying physical reality as illusion, they deny it the dignity of other forms of spirit; it is seen as something to be escaped, to be left behind as one ascends spiritually.

But what if we were to reverse this thinking? What if we were to deny any separation between matter and spirit by suggesting that everything is matter? In terms of Occam's Razor and the experience gained through life and observation, this would appear to be the most sensible conclusion, the one which is most in accord with Reality as we know it. It certainly seems to be a good foundation to build upon; if other planes, distinct from the physical, do exist, the onus is upon them to prove themselves. This is the position taken by the Church of Satan, who stress the carnal nature of Reality.

You may argue that thoughts are not material things,

that emotions are not material things, that our wild imaginings are things beyond the physical world. This is balderdash. Our thoughts and our imaginings and our emotions all occur within our physical brains. They don't occur in some other reality, they occur here and now. It's simply that these things – generally assumed to be purely subjective, or spiritual – have always been considered to be separate from matter. But there is no reason why we should suppose this to be so. Even the attribution of Spirit or consciousness to the fifth Elemental point of the Pentagram indicates that this is so: according to the attributions of this ancient occult symbol, Spirit is just as much a part of the manifest Universe as Fire, Water, Air and Earth (or, respectively, energy, liquid, gas and solid, the states of matter). The only change we need to make in order to establish this unified model is accept that consciousness suffuses matter and is an aspect of it. We ourselves are evidence of this.

When this notion that "all is matter" takes root, it implies two things with regard to magical practice. Firstly, the magician's training must begin with the body and the five physical senses, exactly as in the *APOPHIS* curriculum. Secondly, the other worlds and realms of the astral plane that we discussed in the previous chapter can now be clearly interpreted as having a very real and tangible existence, but that existence is within the consciousness of the magician; it is not some 'place' on 'another plane' that you can go to. It is an inward journey. What does this imply about the otherworldly entities, spirits and gods that are met in these regions? We'll consider the ramifications of this in the next chapter.

There are a couple of protestations that people are bound to make at this point. Some might argue that their thoughts cannot possibly be part of the material world because they do not influence reality. Well, of course they do! Every single thing you do is done because you have thought to do so.

You choose which thoughts to put into action, but they are all real and contain the potential to affect the world. You cannot pick up your coffee cup without first issuing a mental impulse to do so. As for your more outlandish conceptions, such as pastel green unicorns, you may not see such creatures cantering around the fields, but you can certainly tangibly sculpt one or paint one, or tell a story about one. And the image is composed of colours and shapes and notions that exist in the material world, even if not in this precise configuration. The error here is failing to realise that creativity too is a quality of matter. It makes no odds whether you create something like a palace or a garden fence, or incredible fantasy vistas within your own mind; there is no distinction when you recognise that mind and matter are ultimately the same substance. They just have different degrees of subjectivity and objectivity; but subjective and objective here are mere relational markers, not exclusive absolutes. Objectivity is simply the degree to which an event is measurable by another person. Wailing that "I can't levitate a table by thinking about it!" is no argument, it's simply wrong application of force. You can't levitate a table by switching on your car engine either, which is another way of saying exactly the same thing. But you **can** levitate a table by putting it in the boot of your car, then turning the key and driving off with it, just as you **can** levitate a table by thinking about it and then subsequently moving your limbs to walk across and lift it off the ground with your hands. All of these things are on the same plane and thus able to relate.

Some readers will by now be beginning to think that this is a very narrow and materialistic view of life. But we are seekers after truth, so this shouldn't be a problem, surely? If this is the way things are, then this is the way things are. And I am certainly not denying the power of magic, I am simply destroying some of the false premises often used to explain it.

For such readers, all I can say is that you will have to wait until I start to rebuild a new and clear magical vision and worldview in the *coagula* section of the book. In the meantime, we still have a lot of deconstruction left to do.

Other readers may by now have started to intuit where I'm ultimately heading with all of this and may be beginning to get excited about it. If so, congratulations on your perceptiveness. You will have realised by now that the discovery of this 'single plane' model of Reality is going to demand a rethink of definitions of matter and consciousness. But for the moment we are clearing away the smoke and mirrors, not reconstructing the truth.

## Of Gods and Spirits

Magicians habitually hobnob with gods, spirits, angels, demons and assorted otherworldly beings on a regular basis. And to be fair, there is already much debate among practitioners of magic concerning the reality of these beings, even before I start poking my paddle in the waters.

Even the very best minds have struggled with this question, and have often changed their minds over the years. In Aleister Crowley's younger years, when he published the Mathers translation of the *Goetia*, adding his own introduction to it, he argued that the conjured spirits were projections from the magician's own subconscious. If a magician wished to seduce someone, he would find a suitable spirit in the grimoire and perform his evocation. But what he would actually call forth was an aspect of his innermost self, usually submerged below the threshold of consciousness. This aspect would embody his charisma, personal magnetism and sex appeal, awakening these forces within him so that when he attempted his seduction, he would stand a much greater chance of success.

In later years, Crowley came to believe the opposite to be true, considering that the spirits might be literal independent entities. At the very least, he believed in the literal existence of the Deities of the *Book of the Law*: Nuit, Hadit, Horus, Babalon and his Holy Guardian Angel Aiwass. But in his magnum opus *Magick*, his manual of practical magical instruction, he wrote the following: *"In this book it is spoken of...Spirits and Conjurations; of Gods, Spheres, Planes and many other things which may or may not exist. It is immaterial whether they exist or not. By doing certain things certain results follow."*

The position in the Temple of Set is not set in stone, the question being left to the understanding of each Initiate. The official position is that Set Himself is an objectively existing entity, and this is the position which all members of the Priesthood are expected to hold. But even that is a supposition with many possible interpretations. Temple members in general are not required to adhere to this opinion. Concerning other Gods and spirits, the matter is again largely left to personal opinion. Some hold the other Egyptian Deities – the *Neteru* – to possess individual, objective existence; others don't. Others believe that most Gods are the personification of natural forces, with spirits such as those of the *Goetia* being assumed to be products of the human psyche, symbolic personifications of the nature described by Crowley in his *Goetia.*

In the Church of Satan, Anton LaVey defined Satan as the "dark force in nature" which drives human evolution and genius, bringing about necessary change in opposition to crushing conformity. Satan was thus a metaphor for the awakened human spirit, but a lively one and one which could seem to take on a life of its own. The other diabolical names and beings called upon in Satanic rituals were specialised aspects of this same dark genius within, called forth to awaken and enable the desired qualities.

I have discussed the question of what precisely spirits are at great length in the lectures of The Apophis Club and here is not the place to go into such precise and convoluted discussions. We will return to discuss this matter further towards the end of the *coagula* section, but for now, in our work of deconstruction, the perspective of the Church of Satan seems to be the most likely and workable scenario. This also accords with our law that nearly all magical phenomena have no supernatural element. This means that most spirit encounters (whether by astral meeting or ritual conjuration) are projections from the deep places of the magician's psyche. They remain powerful forces, but are not externally independent entities.

## Mediums and Psychics

Talk of spirits may make our minds wander away from questions of gods and dæmons and consider instead the spirits of the dead, together with the mediums and psychics who claim to be able to communicate with them.

I'm going to put aside the question of whether there is life after death for now. It suffices for the moment to say that it's not something that can be proven, and that if there is, we would need to spend some considerable time defining what kind of life it could be. And still it would not be proven. Therefore, this is a philosophical matter best held over until the third part of the book, after we have deconstructed magic and rebuilt a coherent model around which to weave our speculations.

So for the time being we must set aside that part of the question for later and instead concentrate upon the question that **if** spirits of the dead **do** exist, is it possible to communicate with them? Are mediums and psychics fraudulent or genuine, or a mix of both?

I have sat in the audience and watched a fair few mediums at work in my time, some famous and others definitely not so. I can say, hand on heart, that I have **never** witnessed a single genuine mediumistic demonstration. The identification of both spirits and sitters is shoddy and the 'messages' passed on are so pathetic as to be laughable, if it were not for the fact that there are poor, bereaved people sitting in the audience desperate to believe this tripe and be momentarily reunited with their loved ones.

Perhaps this may be best demonstrated by quoting from memory some of the bullshit I heard at one meeting:

*"Does anybody know someone whose name began with a D? I'm getting a D, could be a father or a brother ... do you remember anything about a budgie? Did you used to have a budgie, or was there a budgie somewhere around, maybe at a friend's or a relative's? ... Ah, it must be you, then. Yes, he says that's right, he's got a message for you: he sends you love..."*

This old fraud waffled on in the same manner for about an hour and a half. He kept pulling out the same old hooks; I forget how many times he asked people if they knew anyone who had ever had a budgie. At no time did the information offered become more specific than the above. An awful lot of additional information was volunteered to him by the audience, who were convinced he was the real deal, but none of it originated with him.

There was a family present, two parents with their two daughters. I recognised the parents as people who circulate through nearly all of the local psychic events, true believers both. Evidently one of the daughters was having as much difficulty as me accepting all of this bullshit. The way in which the medium sidelined her was devious and cunning; he suggested that the reason she found his gift so hard to accept was that she herself was similarly gifted and was afraid of the fact. This immediately made the audience nod and feel compassion for her, completely patronising her, because she was unable to "accept her gift", which his mighty insight had so clearly discerned. Her parents looked so proud about this, that poor girl's life must have been a misery afterwards as they pestered her to develop her non-existent clairvoyant talents. This was a cold and merciless trick by a cheat, but I have to give him grudging admiration for the way in which he accomplished it, instantly bringing the audience on his side, turning a sceptic into an asset, taking away their credibility whilst seeming to praise them.

There are no genuine mediums. None at all. It is all trickery or self-delusion. I've seen some who obviously believe what they do; in fact, they're embarrassing in their desperation to believe, but so usually are their audiences, so they all feed back into each other and go home convinced. The more polished shows are actively fraudulent.

If the dead do communicate with the living, it's not like this. It simply does not happen. We'll come back to look at other methods of post-mortem communication before we close this chapter, but first let's take a look at professional psychics.

You guessed it, these too are frauds, using cold-reading techniques, stooges, selective memory and so forth to fake it. Again, some evidently genuinely believe that their random thoughts and whims are psychic communications and will happily let all manner of garbage trip off their tongue; others are deliberately conning you, using vague prompts to elicit information. And they are all somehow qualified to teach their gifts, you notice, offering expensive courses which even the most inept pass with flying colours after paying the astronomical fees. I have a friend who has racked up hundreds and hundreds of pounds of credit card debt attending these 'seminars' that he can't afford to repay, and there are many, many more like him. All of this despite the fact he knows of my magical history and I continually warn him not be fooled, but like so many, he is **desperate** to believe, against all evidence to the contrary.

I'm simply stating these things for the record, of course. Any magician worth his salt already knows these things, because anybody with any kind of **genuine** psychic experience will know damn well that it doesn't happen to order like this. Not ever. Anybody who says it does is a liar, a con man, or a fool.

Genuine magicians understand that psychic and clairvoyant phenomena are not produced to order, and when they do happen they are generally accompanied by a definite physical sensation (a cue which is soon recognised by the magician) and they only last scant seconds. Each such phenomenon must be accepted on its own terms; the information 'received' is inevitably accurate, but all attempts to elongate the experience or seek out more than came through of its own accord always leads to false assumptions and imaginary details which are proved wrong after checking. To stand in front of an audience and make the claims that mediums and professional psychics do is at best self-deceit on a colossal scale, or more likely deliberate, malicious fraud.

For those who are interested, if you search on Amazon, you will find a large selection of books which will teach you all of the tricks employed by mediums and professional psychics, all the way from simple cold-reading to how to duplicate the table-turning and spirit materialisation antics of the Victorian mediums.

Yet, I have intimated above that although more fleeting and less showy in nature, genuine psychic phenomena do occur. So after dismissing all the bullshit, what lies behind these genuine occurrences, with which the magician will no doubt become personally familiar?

The mechanism is a simple one to describe: such a psychic breakthrough occurs at a moment when the brain is 'idling' and the conscious and subconscious are able to briefly connect. The magician experiences a jolt, a physical response, and then the flash is over. Basically, as soon as your attention snaps back to focus upon the thing, the usual gap between conscious and subconscious is immediately reinstated. This is the dilemma; you can only recognise and respond to such a flash of inspiration / insight by effectively cutting it off. But your subconscious is not stupid, and what you receive will be what you need.

So what is it that actually happens? Do two minds actually connect to share information, or is the psyche able to discern things at a distance and convey something to the magician that he should not have otherwise been able to know? In some cases in my experience, there have been incidents which only seem explicable in such terms. However, although such things do seem able to happen, you shouldn't at this stage (or any) simply take my word for that, and in any case such otherwise inexplicable incidences seem to be in the definite minority. Most such incidents can be explained by the transmission of information from the subconscious to the conscious levels of awareness which has been previously noticed and filed away by the brain, but beneath the threshold of conscious awareness. The subconscious basically reaches out to inform the magician of something important that it has noticed, but his conscious mind has missed. This knowledge seems to miraculously spring up in the brain, as if from nowhere, a sudden remarkable realisation. But again our rule holds true: in most cases, although a remarkable incidence of conscious / subconscious communication and thus noteworthy in its own right, no supernatural element need be inferred to have been involved.

Before concluding this chapter, we need to briefly consider another means of communing with the dead, this being the more controlled and potent method of necromancy, a method practised by magicians with due precision, skill and

Will, a far cry from the mediums' shenanigans.

Readers who who have dipped into many of my Apophis Club publications may recall that in the book *Gods and Monsters* I gave a detailed account of my necromantic conjuration of the shade of Dr John Dee, the Elizabethan magician. More details on the substance of these conjurations were later given in the book *The Sevenfold Mystery*.

So what can be learned from the experience of necromancy? Firstly, let's ask our default question: did the experiment actually work? The answer is yes, I successfully – and very fruitfully, as *The Sevenfold Mystery* proves – conversed with Dee's shade.

The question then becomes: what then is this shade? Is it literally the dead person's spirit and personality? The answer in this case, however, is no.

The shade is something which is left behind when a person dies and departs the world. It is, if you like, the imprint that the person has made upon the world, and most specifically the imprint he has made upon the minds that knew him. As such, at least a part of that imprint consists of people's memories. We have to consider the possibility – if not the probability – that much of what constitutes an evoked shade is a simple shadow play of memories and reflections within our own minds. With an individual such as Dee, this shade may endure for many centuries, as his imprint has been great and he is still often thought of by magicians.

If you would like a second example of a magician's necromantic experiment, read the account of Eliphas Levi's evocation of the shade of Apollonius of Tyana in his *Transcendental Magic*. Apollonius' shade, being far further removed across the centuries, his life less well known in its details, was very nebulous when called.

But in either case, a conjured shade is never the true essence of the person. It has no consciousness *per se*, only memory and reflection. Nevertheless, in its interactions with the subconscious of a skilled magician, it may reveal many secrets and profound insights. *The Sevenfold Mystery* stands as testament to this fact.

So what does this leave us with? That once again our rule seems to hold true, and the the supernatural need not be invoked as an explanation in nearly all necromantic experiences.

## The Higher Self

Most magical traditions speak of a so-called 'Higher Self'. It may be called by all manner of names, such as the Holy Guardian Angel, the Augoeides, the Dæmon. But almost all commentators reference this 'Higher Self' at some point. And very, very many of them are content to spout utter and total bollocks about it, filling learning magicians' minds with bullshit.

The Self is a complex and multi-faceted thing. Every magical tradition agrees with this; psychology agrees with this. There is far more to a person than the muted automaton who works, eats, shits and sleeps. Every human being has passions and desires, visions and aspirations, capable of great creativity and genius. These qualities are suppressed by the workaday world, and advertising and the media do their level best to channel these urges to the places where they will engender the most profit for others, such as fashion, popular entertainment and so on.

The Higher Self – or the Dæmon as it is called in the context of The Apophis Club – is quite simply the true Genius of the Self awakened and brought fully to life and consciousness. In other words, it is the development and celebration of our own creativity, our own wishes and desires, our own sense of values, ethics and aesthetics. This may seem like a small thing, but it requires a literal inner revolution to overthrow the bonds of advertising and conformity. The liberation of the Dæmon, the true Creative Self, is the most empowering and liberating thing imaginable.

But there are another set of chains that we have to escape first, and these are much more insidious and subtle, but far more dangerous and entrapping for that. The occult attracts many people who have realised how programmed by the media and politics their lives have become; they seek ways to liberate themselves from these externally imposed confines. But very few of them realise that they must also struggle to shatter the chains of occult conformity too.

Because the simple truth is that there are a huge number of people out there who will tell you in no uncertain terms what your Higher Self is, and how you should behave if you want to access it. As if **they** could possibly know **your** personal, innermost nature! And surprise, surprise, their definition of the Higher Self never fails to be just another rehash of the same old tedious, pseudo-Christian moralising, utter bullshit which has neither relevance nor power to your true Self. I have even heard this sort of drivel from people who claim to be Left-Hand Path teachers.

It can be very difficult for new magicians to notice this new set of chains: after all, when the group or person who taught them how to liberate themselves from the shackles that bind most of society, they're going to trust those people when they coax them into a new set of shackles.

But there are two very clear and apparent ways to recognise this and to shrug off such conditioning. Firstly, your Higher Self is **<u>your</u> Higher Self**. Not somebody else's, not some group's or teacher's, just yours. Never let anybody else tell you who or what your Higher Self is, or what its attributes are, or what it wants you to do, or how it wants you to behave. Only **you** can determine that, only **you** have access to your Higher Self. And this rule applies to me and to The Apophis Club as well. Don't accept what I have to say about these things just because I say so. I may be wrong. I may be lying. Don't just accept it as a matter of faith; put my words to the test. Subject them to scrutiny. If what I have to teach is appealing to you, it must be because my words make sense to you after proper consideration, not simply because I wrote them in a book.

The main thing that has to be remembered about your Higher Self is that it is indeed a part of your Self. It is a part of your consciousness and gets its name through being the part that is most awake, aware and integrated. It is presented as something to be aspired to and invoked because it is an image of how we want our entire Self to become in due course, as a result of our magical Work. But it is still your Self, your consciousness. And this means that it is something which has a great affinity with the rest of you. It is not an isolated thing, it is not an alien or an outside deity to be worshipped and obeyed, to be grovelled to whilst it pronounces commandments. It is you and it is the same essence as you.

There are those who claim that the Higher Self is some sort of Christ-like figure and that we must give up everything in order to approach it. As if we are to become ascetics, crawling in sackcloth and ashes, in order to approach the most fully conscious aspect of our own Self. What kind of rubbish is this? I have seen magicians piously give up all of their passions and interests, living like monks because they believe this will be pleasing to their Higher Self. Bullshit! Your passions and interests are **your** passions and interests; therefore they are the **same** as the passions and interests of your Higher Self!

The only thing the magician need give up are the

over-consumerism and slavery promoted by the kind of society we live in. In other words, you cut loose those things that have been put there from outside yourself. In the Apophis curriculum, this is all part of the Work of the first four Heads of the Dragon. But then, in the Fifth Head, as the Dæmon arises into full consciousness within the magician, a concerted and deliberate attempt is made – having wiped the slate clean to remove pre-conditioning – to rediscover and immerse oneself in all of the things that one is passionate about. And I'm not just talking about 'occult' or 'spiritual' things, I mean every delight you ever genuinely felt. If you love moving tiny soldiers on a table, playing tabletop wargames, your Higher Self will love it too – because it is you! Creativity and art and imagination, and the appreciation and passion for these things, are all among the very highest consciousness, so indulge yours and be glad! Because those who fall into the ascetic trap are every bit as much a slave as they were when they set out.

I received a review on Amazon recently for my book *Ægishjálmur*, which made my eyebrows raise and proved this point very well, as the reviewer very obviously simply didn't 'get it'. He wrote as follows: *"For the most part the author is structuring his book on the concept that we are to gain control over our lower selves (dragon within) in order to harness our desire energy towards awakening the Wode-Self. While this is a classic hook in today's world, promising that we can continue down our lower nature's desired roads without having to change, what ends up happening, especially when all we have is the little bit of self-control work the author offers, is a false sense of power that ultimately becomes our downfall as our lower natures do what they do best: please themselves at the expense of the rest of our self."* This is all very pious and neo-Christian and falls into that same old trap of assuming that there is some moral duality separating the Higher Self and the so called 'lower nature'. It's just another Remanifestation that those of us born in nations that have been infected with the poison of the desert religions are indoctrinated into from birth. The desires of the 'lower self' are the same as the desires of the 'Higher Self'; the only distinction is the Will and power available to achieve those goals and the improved balance factor and far sight of a more unified consciousness. The goal of Initiation is to integrate the **whole** Self, not to suppress or deny part of it, for as soon as you fall into this trap you stop short at best or fall back into guilt and neurosis at worst.

So embrace the Vision of the Higher Self and seek to unify all parts of your consciousness into a single perfect sublimity. But you will still be wonderful, glorious you! The people who fall and who experience self-destructive tendencies are those who fail to achieve this integration, denying their very own natures. And never forget that the Apophis curriculum – as all genuine initiatory paths – starts with the realisation that we are carnal creatures and that all of our levels of conscious awareness must spring from that foundation.

Perhaps one day someone may succeed in inventing a time machine and will go back to put a bullet through that old lunatic Abraham's head, before any of the guilt-ridden, murderous, psychotic religions the crazy old fool spawned have time to appear.

## The Healing Arts

Magical healing and various other kinds of 'alternative' healing are also things surrounded by superstitions and unwarranted beliefs. More alarmingly, genuine, effective medicines often bear the brunt of occultists' hostility on social media these days, as if science was somehow 'the enemy'.

I shouldn't have to mention exploitative faith healers, as they've been pretty much covered whilst discussing fraudulent mediums. Exactly the same applies here. There is nothing more despicable than these vampires who prey on the desperately sick for money, offering them false hope and lies, then often having the nerve to blame the victim for not having enough faith when the 'cure' fails.

I also lump into the same category those idiots who genuinely believe that they channel healing energies through Reiki or other such nonsense. **It. Does. Not. Fucking. Work.** I know people who practise Reiki, I have experienced it at their hands, I have witnessed them use it on others. I have heard all the stuff about symbols and energy. It is utter bullshit and it heals nothing. It may be a superb Lesser Magical technique in the hands of a skilled showman to assist in the alleviation of pain or symptoms (we'll get back to this shortly), but it does nothing to heal any underlying illness or injury. We can also include other 'alternative healing' techniques, such as acupuncture and homeopathy. They simply do not work, they have no effect upon any ailments. They too may occasionally temporarily lessen symptoms, but never the underlying condition.

And yet when we look at conventional medicine, stuff that does actually make people well, many occultists are rabidly against it. They say it isn't safe, that it isn't natural. If it exists, of course it's bloody natural! Of course, what they actually mean is that it's been refined and prepared by Western scientists instead of picked from the herb garden of a backwater shaman somewhere. They offer up the word 'natural' as if it was a panacea, radiant with love and light. Shall I tell you what's 'natural'? The plague bacillus, that's natural, as is leprosy, as is smallpox. Mmm, all that natural goodness, eh? It is scientists and Western medicine that have eradicated smallpox, produced a cure for leprosy and created the antibiotics that give plague victims a fighting chance. These diseases are now generally limited to those places where Western medicine is least present. Measles too was also almost eradicated, but that's making a huge resurgence now, because of ignorant people refusing to have their children vaccinated.

If you go to any of these places in the world which are still lacking Western medicine, where it is difficult to procure, you won't find the people there raving about the 'natural' cures they have available. **They** want **our** medicine, because they know it's what will make them well!

Claims are made that medicines are toxic, that vaccinations are poisonous, etc. Of course they are! Everything is toxic. **Everything!** The food you eat is toxic, it can kill you. Drink too much water and it will kill you. The very air you breathe is toxic, oxygen is one of the most corrosive substances. The things that keep us alive are paradoxically all toxic. But they don't kill us because of the quantities in which they are taken into our systems. The same is true of medicines, which is why it requires careful measurement and precise prescription by people who know what the hell they are talking about in order to render them both effective and safe. In some cases, such as the stronger forms of chemotherapy, the medicines can be very toxic, with awful side effects. But those side effects are a damn sight better than being dead and these medicines have saved countless lives; they may not be pleasant, but they can be very effective, they offer a real hope, and contrary to what you may read online, this is something that smoking a joint will definitely **not** do (though it may help manage your pain and make you forget your symptoms for a while).

Vaccination is the big elephant in the room these days, of course, with utterly unfounded hysteria claiming that it causes autism. Rubbish. There is no evidence for this at all. None. But you know what? Even if it did have a one in ten thousand chance of causing autism or some such, that would still be vastly preferable to the alternative. Millions upon millions of lives have been saved through vaccination. Diseases that once culled whole populations are under control. These are facts.

The acid test is this: I have met many people who are **only** alive today because of conventional Western medicine, without which they would have died. I myself am one and my wife is another. I have met **nobody** who can say the same about alternative medicine.

So why do some of these alternative treatments appear to work for a short time (and it is only ever for a short time, never a long term improvement)? It's simply down to the placebo effect. The placebo effect was noticed during clinical trials of new drugs; sometimes the control group, taking an inactive compound for sake of comparison, would also report feeling better, though their improvement was never permanent, only apparent, a lessening of symptoms. This occurs because so much of the symptoms that we suffer when ill or injured is within our own minds. And when misdirected away from our illness, the mind is capable of subduing and controlling the worst of the symptoms. Once the fear, focus and anticipation of pain are removed, for example, we find ourselves able to endure far greater extremes of pain without the same anguish. And when a person is led to believe they are being given a treatment which will alleviate their condition, the mind reduces its focus upon the symptoms accordingly, rendering them less intense and more bearable, hence an apparent improvement in the condition. However, the actual illness or injury remains unchanged, we simply become less aware of it.

A similar effect occurs when hypnosis is used to relieve pain; the mind is distracted from it and focused elsewhere, rendering the discomfort negligible or at least significantly more tolerable.

The Lesser Magical applications of healing rites become very apparent when the placebo effect is borne in mind. By his rituals, or amulets, or Reiki or whatever, the magician's charisma works upon the recipient to convince them that they are feeling better. This leads to a tremendous uplift in general positivity and reduces the impact of pain and other symptoms significantly for a greater or lesser period of time. It does not actually heal an illness or injury, however, it provides comfort and the opportunity to rest easily.

What about when a ritual is worked in all earnestness, with a view to a genuine healing? What occurs then? It really does follow the same exact pattern as the principles we have already discussed. It focuses the magician's mind upon the problem, opening awareness to possibilities and opportunities that would otherwise not have been realised. The best doctors will be found, the best surgery performed, the best drugs sourced, because everyone involved will be operating at the top of their game, either directly influenced by a ritual they took part in, or else galvanised and inspired by those who did. But it is the surgery and the doctors and the drugs – plus the body's own immune system – which will actually effect the healing.

What about those cases which seem genuinely impossible, which only a miracle can help? Am I saying then that magic can be of no help in cases such as these? I am only saying for the moment that in nearly all successful rites for magical healing, no supernatural element is involved.

## MAGICAL TOOLS

Every magician has their collection of magical tools. These will vary in details from tradition to tradition, but a few examples will help. Golden Dawn and Thelemite Initiates, for instance, have their four Elemental weapons: a wand for Fire, a chalice for Water, a dagger for Air and a pantacle for Earth. They also have a sword for evocation and a lotus wand for invocation. All consecrated by complex rites and symbolism. All of these tools are supposed to be crafted by the magician's own hand, or at least the final shaping, colouring, marking and consecration should be accomplished personally by the magician. Other tools include such things as Tarot cards, rune sets, talismans that have been created, statuettes and figurines, wall hangings, altars, etc.

We can immediately apply our rule to the question of magical tools. The tools in and of themselves, no matter how artfully created and skilfully consecrated, remain tools. The **process** of creating and consecrating them, the investment of time, intent, Will and imagination in that process, render them very important in the psyche of the magician, however. This is why mass-produced items are so very inferior and it is always better to make your own. That importance in your own mind is deeply ingrained, so when you use these tools in a ritual, they are going to be very powerful keys in unlocking the deep places of your psyche and furnishing the results you want. But in almost all cases, this will be a result of the unique relationship you have established with each object, not an inherent quality of the object itself. In other words this is a little Lesser Magical smoke and mirrors, whereby your own mind's associations empower the object which then empowers your mind.

This Lesser Magical application applies to other people. When they see these hand-crafted tools, adorned with weird sigils and symbolism, they cannot help but feel spooked and in awe of such objects, especially if warned of dire doom should they handle such powerful sacred objects. This raises their expectation that your rituals will produce results and their evident belief increases your own confidence, with the expected knock-on effect.

If you give someone an amulet or talisman that you have made, its image and symbolism will likewise inflame their imagination. Even the sceptical recognise mystical symbols and magical signs and know that they are handling something outside the ordinary. Because in order for the item to be effective and evoke the result you desire, it only has to speak to their subconscious; their conscious scepticism is totally irrelevant where such responses are concerned. When the purpose of the amulet is explained, their subconscious will ensure that it is achieved in order to satisfy its own sense of wonder.

Some tools, such as Tarot cards or rune staves are readily recognised as magically symbolic and most non-magicians experience a *frisson* of supernatural delight upon seeing them. This renders their subconscious completely receptive. Tarot cards in particular can be used to execute a huge number of stage magical type effects, which can be terrifyingly convincing once taken out of the domain of showbiz patter. This in turn prepares the person for further suggestion and priming to achieve your magical purpose.

So magical tools are well worth investing your time and effort in, they can facilitate quite remarkable results. But as in all cases, nearly all successful operations need incorporate no supernatural element.

## The World of Should-Be

One of the major problems facing most new magicians is that they find themselves operating within a World of Should-Be instead of the World That Is.

A magician can only change the world in ways that match his Vision if he first sees and accepts that world exactly as it really is. Otherwise he is working from a false premise and who knows where the hell his ill-informed meddling will lead?

It is necessary to understand the laws of physics, the ways in which the world works. It is also important to understand psychology, the ways in which peoples' minds work. Anybody who wrings their hands and bleats "Why can't we all just get along?" hasn't even **begun** to get this yet. Peoples' major failing is to assume that other people think the same way they do and have the same values that they do. This is manifestly not true.

We will be dealing with the big philosophical questions in section three of this book, including the doozy of why there is evil in the world. But I'm hoping that by the time we get to that point, readers will be well equipped to answer them for themselves. But you owe it to yourself to think about these things in the meantime.

It is human nature to want the whole world to be run along the lines of the snug little enclaves in which the fortunate (such as we in the Western world) find themselves. But the magician needs to understand the realities that underlie the illusion, the ways in which the world actually turns, for nature is indeed red in tooth and claw. In every case, one man's comfort is bought at another man's expense. And I'm not about to sit here and tell you this is a bad thing either. It is up to each of us to make the best of the situation in which we find ourselves and do the best we can for ourselves and our kin. That is nature's way. There are always winners and losers and it's up to you to be a winner, or not. But you can only do that if you understand the rules of the game.

This *solve* section of the book has been deliberately written to shatter your most precious illusions, to toss your superstitions in the garbage, to relegate your beliefs to irrelevance and to deal solely with what we know to be so. Because if you do not establish your magic upon this solid base, you **will** sooner or later fall.

Nature is cruel. Money talks. Might may not be right, but it can certainly act as if it is and get away with it every time. People hate. People kill people. If you don't protect yourself and your loved ones, no one else will if it comes to the test. Face up to it, live with it, deal with it. Stop being surprised by things which are totally predictable. Look Reality in the eye and embrace it for what it is. Then and only then, when you see the World That Is, not the World That Should-Be, will you be in a position to change it and improve it, or at least your small part of it.

MICHAEL KELLY

# COAGULA

## THE IMPORTANCE OF LESSER MAGIC

By deconstructing the processes of magic in the *solve* section of this book, we have placed ourself in a position where all of the beliefs and superstitions have been torn down, where magic has been stripped to its very bones, its rituals and results reduced to a few very down to earth postulates. Armed with this knowledge and clear sight, we are now in a good position to begin the process of reconstruction. None of this reconstruction will nullify any of the sometimes painful realisations that have brought us to this place – if we want to truly be magicians instead of play actors, people who really change the world instead of those who act a role, then we have to do so from a position of understanding what is Real. After dispelling the smoke and mirrors, we have discovered magic to be a very earthbound, carnal thing, rooted in clear behavioural patterns, steered with a cunning mind. There is very little of the mystical or so-called 'spiritual' to be found. However, for the **truly** insightful, those who have stuck with the program and have not cast this book aside in disgust before reaching this point, dismayed at their cherished beliefs getting tossed on the scrap heap, it is just possible that we may discover that the carnal and the cunning are much, much larger things than we ever previously supposed, There is a whole Universe of wonder out there, and it is a Universe that is Real.

One of the first things that will have struck the reader of the *solve* section is just how all-pervasive Lesser Magic actually is. It is not simply a set of techniques for manipulating the viewpoint of others; it is also a means of bewitching our own senses in order to establish a conscious-subconscious connection which is what makes results magic possible. It is a sleight of mind which assists us to see beyond the illusions and presuppositions with which we habitually surround and limit ourselves, so that we can see clearly and achieve the seemingly extraordinary. If there was no more to magic than this, it would still be a worthwhile and rewarding pursuit for these reasons.

So, **is** there more to magic than this? This is something we will discover as we rebuild our magical perspective in this *coagula* section, and we will see what impact our realisations have upon our philosophy in section three, where Kelly will indeed explain Everything – and Nothing.

But first, since we have discovered it to be crucial in one form or another to every magical operation, we need to spend some time on this subject of Lesser Magic. The Key to Lesser Magic in all of its forms can be summarised as follows:

**By persuading somebody that something is true, that person will act as if that something was true, making that something effectively true.**

To give a couple of examples: if you have a project you want to get underway at work and you intimate to others that it was the boss' idea, and then convince the boss it was his idea (not difficult at all to do), your project will be actioned, even if it would have been sidelined if you presented it as your own. Everybody believes it's the boss' baby (including the boss), so suddenly it **is** the boss' baby and gets everyone's full attention.

If you do a ritual to woo and seduce a young lady you regularly see in a night club, the ritual (if you do it properly) will convince you that she is indeed attracted to you. This conviction will give you the confidence and charisma you need in order to actually appear attractive to her.

If you are known to be an effective magician and you prepare a healing talisman for someone who is ill and pass it to them, their confidence in your abilities, reinforced by the strangeness of the talisman, will help their symptoms to abate, allowing them to rest properly and experience some relief. It may also help persuade them and others to ensure the very best medical advice and treatment is being sought.

So Lesser Magical skills are all-pervasive. The techniques of Lesser Magic are far, far too complex and subtle to go into here. An introduction to Lesser Magical techniques can be found in my book *Words of Power*. It is possible to learn Lesser Magic through books and trial and error experimentation, but it really is something that is best taught in person, learning the skills from someone who knows. I will be offering courses in Lesser Magical training once this book has been published. Sign up on the Apophis Club web forum and Facebook page to be sure of getting the details. Orry Whitehand will also shortly be penning a whole series of 'How To...' books which will cover a broad range of specific Lesser Magical techniques. Watch out for those shortly.

Lesser Magic is the great legacy of Anton Szandor LaVey, the founder of the Church of Satan and one of the greatest magicians of the Twentieth Century. Others had certainly practised Lesser Magic before him. Aleister Crowley certainly did. But it wasn't until LaVey came along that someone actually placed these apparent carnival tricks right where they belonged; in the beating heart of genuine occultism. In doing so, he exposed a truth that most occultists try to deny, but which is nonetheless absolutely paramount: **in order to be effective, the magician must be a showman**.

It was LaVey who taught this essential truth: the first and most powerful tool of the magician is **charisma**. In order to Work magic, a magician must possess Will and must be able to direct that Will towards a purpose; he must have Imagination, in order to shape the Unmanifest and give form to his deepest insights; he must have Desire, the fuel that drives him on to change the world. But all of these things are made manifest and communicated through his **charisma**. It is charisma which gives flesh and blood and voice to his magic, which causes the Universe to listen and take heed, which beguiles the unwary and bewitches the listener, weaving visions of wonder that enthrall and fascinate, so that all follow in his wake, like rats or children behind a Pied Piper.

> *"Suddenly another voice spoke, low and melodious, its very sound an enchantment. Those who listened unwearily to that voice could seldom report the words that they had heard; and if they did, they wondered, for little power remained in them. Mostly they remembered only that it was a delight to hear the voice speaking, all that it said seemed wise and reasonable, and desire awoke in them by swift agreement to seem wise themselves. When others spoke, they seemed harsh and uncouth by contrast; and if they gainsaid the voice, anger was kindled in the hearts of those under the spell."*
>
> **- *The Two Towers*, by J.R.R. Tolkien**

# Occult Stage Magic

'Serious' magicians tend to turn their noses up at stage magicians. This is a big mistake. The arts of misdirection and sleight of hand are every bit as magical as the arts of evocation and invocation, and every bit as useful in Working your Will in the world.

Now I'm not recommending necessarily that Draconian magicians should put on a tuxedo and stand in front of an audience asking them to pick a card[3]. Not that there's anything wrong with that, but it's the skills and the approach that we are concerned about learning.

The whole field of stage magic is ripe for study, exploration and practice, practice, practice! But there are four main areas which every Draconian magician can benefit from paying particularly close attention to. We'll deal with each of these in turn.

---

3 Although Paul Fosterjohn, who co-founded The Apophis Club with me right back in its earliest days, did moonlight as a magician. His show was a thing of terror, however, including all manner of macabre effects and culminating in a séance which patrons were known to run from, screaming. It was Paul who introduced me to the ways of the sinister stage showman in earnest.

## 1. Bizarre Magic

Bizarre magic is a very specific sub-genre of stage magic that has appeared in recent years. It is distinguished by the type of effects employed, but also the manner of their presentation.

Bizarre magicians tend to employ effects which are based around disturbing, sinister or occult subjects. They won't use playing cards when Tarot cards are so much more evocative, for instance. They often base their acts around occult routines such as a séance. Some will even work apparent necromantic rituals, with the illusions of spectral apparitions, reworking the routines of Victorian mediums. In my own arsenal, I have several routines using Tarot cards and runes, themes of damnation, effects based around the Faust legend, Jack the Ripper, witch trials and witchfinders' deceits, and so forth. The bizarre magician delves into these dark waters, using occult equipment and produces apparently genuine supernatural phenomena – at least from the perspective of witnesses. It can be seen why these skills would be of benefit to a magician, reinforcing belief in your powers and through that belief perhaps opening the way to genuine manifestations.

The other thing which distinguishes bizarre magic is that there is none of the normal magician's patter. Instead, the bizarre magician is all about presentation and giving a complete performance. The effects he produces are almost secondary to the stories he tells, means of raising the tension, evoking an atmosphere and providing high drama. One effect, titled 'Balnagowne', developed by The Black Hart, tells the story of a Scottish village called Balnagowne where a series of notorious witch trials were carried out. The magician tells the story of these trials and as he does so, he passes around a coffin nail from one of the executed witch's burials, so that a psychic link may be established between his listeners and the victim. He then produces a scroll, which bears a facsimile of the writ of execution relating to this same victim. A list of the accused women is shown and one of the audience then uses a pair of scissors and cuts this list in two at a random point, but unable to see where they are making the cut. The writ is then read and the accused witch is named, revealing that her sentence was to be hanged by the neck and then cut in half. When the list is examined, the audience member is discovered to have cut the same woman's name through the middle, slicing her in two. The magical effect is dramatic and its means are unfathomable, but the spellbinding effect is achieved most of all through story telling. It is this charisma which makes the bizarre magician so different, having people hanging on his every word as he tells his spine chilling tales. Most bizarre magicians deliberately cultivate a sinister stage personality to go with their routine, dressing their space with all manner of occult paraphernalia. It will be readily understood why this kind of magic is very much a demonstration of Lesser Magic at its very finest; the audience fall readily under the magician's spell. These techniques are readily adaptable for off-stage use also.

**2. Divination**

Many bizarre magicians also perform divination routines as part of their shows (these theatrics are best restricted to private functions of 20-30 people, since most bizarre effects are of the close-up variety). They may offer attendees Tarot readings. Some of these may be sleight of hand effects in themselves. Others will be genuine readings, but will be hugely enhanced when the reader demonstrates his psychic ability by gradually revealing the identity of each card before he turns it over as the reading progresses. This will be done subtly, without drawing attention to it, but it will suddenly dawn upon the audience what is occurring, with a thrill of superstitious awe. Naturally, a good deck of marked Tarot cards are essential for this purpose, so that the reader can identify them from their backs. It will be readily understood how much extra weight this 'proof' of clairvoyance gives to a reading, making the recipient pay proper, awe-struck heed to the advice and / or instructions given. This is something which should obviously be in every Lesser Magician's arsenal.

### 3. Mentalism

A particularly fascinating aspect of stage magic is that sub-category which is generally known as mentalism. This refers specifically to those effects which seem to imply mind-reading, as the magician demonstrates knowledge concerning the person he is talking to that he could not possibly know.

Mentalism is something which is effected by a whole range of tricks and techniques, including cold reading, simple research, suggestion and code words. Watch some television shows or Youtube videos featuring masters of the art, such as Derren Brown. Also, read *Practical Mental Magic* by Theodore Annemann, the classic on the art.

It shouldn't be necessary to explain how powerfully effective it can be for the magician to 'prove' his psychic credentials in this way. It was a practice that Aleister Crowley was allegedly very fond of when meeting someone for the first time, to impress them with his power and make them susceptible to further suggestion.

### 4. Suggestion

This is in some respects the flip side of mentalism; whereas mentalism is about extracting information from a subject's mind, suggestion is about putting information in there without them consciously realising it.

In order to plant suggestions effectively, it is necessary to understand a thing or two about hypnosis. For a start, you need to realise what hypnosis actually is, which is simply a distracted or focused attention, in which the mind is looking in upon itself. It is not necessary to enter a 'trance', nor to fall into a 'deep sleep' in order to be hypnotised. You are in a light hypnotic state whilst watching television (easy prey for the advertising!); you are in a hypnotic state while reading this very book.

Once this is realised, you will understand that you can implant suggestions in people's minds while they are fully awake, so long as they do not realise consciously that you are doing it. The suggestions must slip below their guard and go direct to the subconscious.

Suggestions may be verbal or visual, they may be triggered by association with other visual cues or sounds. They will probably have to be subtly built up over time until the subconscious automatically responds without the conscious mind even realising what is happening. The suggestions will probably have to be covert or coded in some way, so as to avoid conscious filtration.

You can find such techniques for suggestion in NLP handbooks, by watching (again) videos of that master of the technique, Derren Brown (check Youtube for his encounter with Simon Pegg, in which he not only carries off a tremendous demonstration of suggestion, but then goes on to explain precisely how he did it), and also check out the remarkable series of books by the Rogue Hypnotist, available from Amazon and worth their weight in gold.

All of these techniques of suggestion and persuasion are supplemented by an arsenal of other factors, such as body language, tone of voice, rhythm of speech, physical appearance, all chosen to reinforce the impression the magician is trying to make.

The usefulness of the first two factors will be adjusted depending upon the type of magician you are and how open you are about your occult interests. In some instances, you may not wish to present yourself as a literal magician. But in all cases, you will benefit from learning the bizarre magician's story telling technique and the production of props to reinforce your words at precise points in the narrative. No other magic is as powerful as the magic of a well told story, delivered with charisma and style; it can reshape opinions and rubber stamp decisions like nothing else can.

Even in instances where you do not utilise standard divination techniques, you can learn to adapt spreadsheets and statistics into divinatory tools, using the diviner's spiel to impose your own interpretations and slant upon data in a coherent and persuasive manner. This is supplemented by mentalist techniques, where you always appear to be one step ahead, impressing those you work with by the way in which you always have your finger on the pulse, seemingly aware of all that transpires before anyone else has told you. Whose advice do you think they are going to trust and follow when you demonstrate such skills? The use of suggestion needs no further explanation.

It's not all about influencing others in order to get what you want, of course. A thorough working knowledge of these techniques also enhances your Medial and Greater Magical practices. The more you can create a mysterious atmosphere for yourself, the more immersed in your magical process your imagination becomes, and the more effective the ritual. You need powerful story telling techniques in order to make your invocations effective, carrying your concentration and passion along for the ride, bridging that gap between conscious and subconscious, which is key to all successful magic.

## By Force of Will Alone

Throughout all of the currents that have swirled through the world of magical practice since the days of the Golden Dawn, we find this theme recurring – even in the midst of tomes devoted to details of ritual practice – that magic can and must be ultimately Worked by pure Will. Crowley wrote of this. All of the tools, the invocations, the beliefs, all of these things are but window dressing, evocative and effective but not the smoking gun. It is Will and Will alone which is the operative force in magic. This was made explicit in 'The Statement of Belial', one of the sections of a document entitled *The Diabolicon*, which was written by Dr Michael Aquino whilst a member of the Church of Satan, prior to his establishment of the Temple of Set. *The Diabolicon* mirrored the tale of Milton's *Paradise Lost*, examining the various Satanic archetypes and their rebellion against stasis and non-consciousness. Belial, whose name means 'without a master', spoke of the fully evolved Black Magician, an individual termed the Black Magus, whose magic was of the uttermost purity. Devoid of props and incantations and other paraphernalia, the Black Magus called upon neither God nor Dæmon, but Worked his magic "by force of Will alone", simply by bringing his own mind to bear upon a situation in order to change it.

During my time in the Temple of Set, Ipsissimus James Lewis penned a document titled 'The Chicago Letter'. This letter was addressed to attendees at one of the Temple's regional Conclaves and proved to be a very controversial statement at the time. In it, James Lewis suggested that the time had surely come for Black Magicians to cease calling upon things which never were, to stow the black robes and other paraphernalia away in the attic where it belongs and to stride forth to practice their magic in the clear light of day, devoid of superstition.

He was right, you know. I have devoted my Work since that time to making this far-sighted Vision a reality, identifying the precise Keys and processes which make magic feasible. These are the things which we shall be examining in this *coagula* section of the book.

The *solve* third of the book was an act of deliberate deconstruction, which has hopefully shown just how true this proposition is. Our magic does not work by calling upon Gods or Fiends or Spirits of any description; the robes and wands and seals and sigils are all so much stage dressing, a way of weaving a compelling story, spellbinding others (or ourselves) with our Lesser Magic, but not in themselves a conduit for change.

We have seen how effective and all-pervasive Lesser Magic is, but we have realised that all of these things are means of manipulation, of triggering a response. The only thing ultimately compelling such magical change is the Will that drives us to accomplish it.

Throughout this book, I have asserted the rule that nearly all successful magical Workings contain no supernatural element. This was not hypothetical rhetoric, designed for shock value purposes. After three decades of magical practice (and half of that time as a Master Recognised by my peers), that is precisely the situation as I see it.

Careful readers will have realised long ago that I am in no way denying the reality or the power of magic. Witness that I have very carefully used the phrase "successful magical Workings" when formulating my rule. I would hardly have done that if I believed that magic does not work, or that it is simply self-delusion. Magic **does** work and it is a very powerful tool, but we need to learn to comprehend it in a new way, devoid of superstition and unfounded suppositions.

These same careful readers will also have noticed that in each case when I have invoked this rule, I have been careful to cite **almost** or **nearly** all. What of those elusive few instances which do not fit into the 'almost all'? Am I therefore saying that there **are** some rare occasions when magic has no other channel to manifest through than one which appears to be supernatural, contrary to the laws of physics?

Now that we have entered the *coagula* phase of the book and are in process of reconstructing magic from the building blocks we have identified, all of its past accretions and detritus swept away, I can cease to be deliberately provocative and we can begin to address these questions from a standpoint of objective knowledge and analysis, not superstition. But in order to do so, we will need to face up to the very real implications of all that we discovered in the *solve* phase, and this will necessitate a new and very different model of Reality.

The clue to this lies in the insistence I made that there is no differentiation between matter and spirit (as they are usually called). They are a single substance. I knew when I wrote this in the *solve* section that most people would interpret it in one of two ways, both equally erroneous. Some would assume it was a statement that the whole Universe is an illusion, that there is no tangible reality; others would assume that it was a statement of total materialism, denying the existence of the 'spirit world'. In point of fact, I said neither of these things. In fact, I specifically said that these two things are exactly the same and of the same 'substance'. We'll come back to this in three or four chapters' time as we have some other matters we need to explore first, but it's a worthwhile distinction to point out to you first, so that you can get your own minds mulling over the issue. For now, consider that if magic is Worked by force of Will, then that Will must be capable of acting upon the substance of the world, thus must necessarily be resonant with that substance, a party to its being.

## Runes For Sceptics

Before we investigate further, I need to demonstrate effectively that such factors as belief and faith have no necessary place in the practice of magic. This is because magic does not require belief in any kind of supernatural agent in order to be wholly effective. All it requires is knowledge, learned skill and application, and confidence in oneself, helped along with a good dose of charisma. In order to illustrate this point, I am devoting this chapter to an explanation of how a complete materialist may Work magic using the runes, without belief in any Gods or Spirits or other supernatural agents. Please note that I am not dismissing discussion of these things, we will reconstruct our view of Spirits etc. later. But the purpose of this chapter is to demonstrate that they are not required for the successful practice of magic. This will help to show how personal Will is indeed the sole effective factor, not any other entity, and will also help to shed light on this unified matter / spirit Universe I am touting (and which will be discussed properly later).

Let's begin by listing the meanings of the twenty four runes of the Elder Futhark:

| ***Rune*** | ***Meaning*** | ***Inner Principle*** |
|---|---|---|
| ᚠ Fehu | Fire, Cattle, Gold | Expansion, Heat, Financial Exchange |
| ᚢ Uruz | Aurochs | Ferocity, Physical Vitality |
| ᚦ Thurisaz | Thurs, Giant | Obstruction, Brute Force |
| ᚨ Ansuz | Ancestral Sovereign God / Odin | Wisdom, Speech, Ecstasy, Inspiration |
| ᚱ Raidho | Riding, Wagon | Journey, Right Action |
| ᚲ Kenaz | Torch, Flame | Applied Energy, Controlled Fire |
| ᚷ Gebo | Gift | Exchange, Act of Giving |
| ᚹ Wunjo | Joy | Joy, Fellowship |
| ᚺ Hagalaz | Hail | Hail, Destruction & Renewal, Seed Form |
| ᚾ Nauthiz | Need | Necessity, Resistance |
| ᛁ Isa | Ice | Ice, Contraction |
| ᛃ Jera | Year | Annual Cycle, |

| | | |
|---|---|---|
| | | Harvest |
| ᛇ Eihwaz | Yew | Yew Tree, Yggdrasil, Life & Death |
| ᛈ Perthro | Lot Cup | Luck, Chance |
| ᛉ Elhaz | Elk | Divine Protection, Aspiration |
| ᛊ Sowilo | Sun | Glory, Clear Guidance, Courage |
| ᛏ Tiwaz | Tyr | Rectitude, Honour, Victory, Cosmic Axis |
| ᛒ Berkano | Birch | Mother, Growth, Protection, Nurture |
| ᛖ Ehwaz | Horse | Partnership, Marriage, Loyalty |
| ᛗ Mannaz | Man | Consciousness, Humanity, Mortality |
| ᛚ Laguz | Lake | Water, Crossing Point, Rite of Passage |
| ◇ Ingwaz | Ing | Earth God, Seed, Fertility, Hidden |
| ᛞ Dagaz | Day | Day / Night, Opposites, Paradox |

| | | |
|---|---|---|
| ᛟ Othila | Home, Enclosure | Fixed Wealth, Homestead, Security |

One of the first things that we can discern by studying the above list is that the runes all have concrete, readily understandable meanings. They either refer to something tangible, such as cattle, the Sun or a yew tree, or they refer to a readily understood concept, experience or emotion, such as joy, or a year. The inner principles which lie behind these rune meanings are likewise easy to understand. Everyone knows what is meant when we talk of finance, or necessity, or motherhood, or ferocity.

So if I turn around to a complete sceptic and say, "We have here twenty four runes, which are each a kind of shorthand for the things and the principles that they represent. If you spend time memorising these runes and their shades of meaning, you will give yourself an easy way of cataloguing these aspects of reality, which you will then be able to bring back to mind in all their fullness simply by seeing or thinking upon the shape or sound of the rune." That sceptical person will find little reason to find fault with what I have said. By spending time to learn the runes, they will provide themselves with powerful mnemonic keys to bring these meanings back to mind. There is nothing ooga-booga or make-believe about this, everything is grounded in what can be seen, felt and experienced by any rational person. So far, so good.

If this sceptic then worked hard at internalising the runes, their meanings and principles, until they provoked automatic subconscious recall and recognition, they would then find no difficulty in agreeing with me when I pointed out that we had now installed brain software which would categorise and assess internal and external phenomena and impressions. For instance, if they took a car journey, they would think *raidho*; if they saw the Sun in the sky, they would think *sowilo*; if they gave a present to their spouse, they would think *gebo*; if they flicked a light switch, channelling electricity to illuminate a room, they would think *kenaz*. And all of these associations would occur naturally and instantly, purely by dint of them having learned the attributes of the runes. There is nothing supernatural about any of this.

But what if I wanted to teach this sceptic how to work magic? Would such a thing be possible? All I would have to do is point out to him that since the runes were now encoded in his subconscious, he could use them to bring into conscious consideration all manner of insights and bright ideas that might not otherwise have occurred to him. All he would need to do in order to achieve this would be to encode a suitable message in runes; these runes would then cross the conscious-subconscious divide and bring forth the desired deep level response.

For example, let's say our sceptical runeworker is short of money. He will struggle to pay the rent this month unless he somehow manages to remedy a shortfall in his cash flow. So he takes a small piece of paper or wood and writes upon it the following runes:

ᚠ ᚾ ᛟ ᛈ ᚠ

*Fehu* bookends the design, emphasising his need for money. *Othila* has the central position, because the purpose of the required funds is the security of his home; he needs to pay the rent. *Othila* is flanked on one side by *nauthiz*, emphasising that this money is requested out of genuine need, not flippantly; on its other side is *perthro*, calling upon the opportunities to fulfil this need.

The sceptical runeworker then smears the prepared runes with a tiny amount of his own blood. This invests himself in the process and asserts his responsibility for the runes he has written. A gesture of this sort is not lost upon the subconscious. He then sings the rune names as he stares at the prepared paper or wood, sending his request deeper into his subconscious as he does so. When he feels ready, he burns the paper or wood to ashes, symbolically removing the matter from his conscious fretting and relying upon his subconscious to furnish the solution. This it will invariably do. Within the next two or three days, he may recall some forgotten item hidden in the loft that he may sell to raise the needed money. Or his senses may simply be more open to opportunities which are always around him in his daily life, but which he normally pays no heed to. Someone needs to hire temporary bar staff perhaps? Or he realises he has some skill that others are willing to pay for which he has never previously considered? We are all surrounded by a multitude of such opportunities every day, but we make a point of ignoring them because usually they don't matter and we have other things on our minds. But his subconscious now jumps to the task, alerting him to these things which are usually filtered out of his awareness. If it judges that his short term shortfall is symptomatic of a longer term problem, it may even give him the necessary nudges to effect a more permanent change in circumstances. But if done properly, the magic **will** work. And he doesn't have to believe in a single supernatural element; he need only believe in his own psychology.

We can also convince our sceptic of the value of divination. We would emphasise that he doesn't have to believe in the significance of which runes fall where, he doesn't have to buy into any concept of fate, nor need he believe the future to be fixed. All that he has to accept is his own natural ability to extrapolate the likelihood of various scenarios from the data he sees playing out in the world around him. His subconscious notices the patterns of events and the ways in which those events are naturally unfolding. He will no doubt accept that his conscious mind tends to miss these important cues, being too wrapped up in the other business of his daily life. Thus, at those times when he needs to perceive and interpret these patterns, he does not know how to recall them or consider them. The runes can assist him in doing so.

The simple fact of laying out runes according to a pre-determined, meaningful pattern, will open his access to his subconscious thought processes. It really doesn't matter which rune falls in which place, because **any** rune will cause his conscious mind to begin looking at his situation from a fresh perspective and cannot fail to provide new insights or food for thought. It really is as simple as that, and whether you personally believe that the precise fall of the runes in a reading is supernaturally significant or not, it is in this spirit that I advise divination should always be approached.

For our current purposes, I am going to pose a random question. So let's assume our sceptic has been invited to visit a friend who resides in a city in a foreign country. He hasn't seen his old friend for far too long, but is worried because the news has recently featured several reports on unrest and rioting in the city in question. His government has advised caution when visiting the region. He is nervous about whether he should go and needs to consider the matter more deeply. Having decided upon a hypothetical question for our sceptic to pose to the runes, I'm now going to draw three completely random runes in a simple three rune spread, representing respectively the root of the matter, the present situation, and the outcome. The three runes selected are as follows:

## ᚾ ᚹ ᛁ

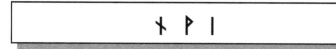

*Nauthiz* is the foundation of our sceptic's dilemma: it repesents necessity and may speak of both the need to see his old friend, but also the need to keep himself safe. It also highlights the rune's meaning of resistance, as the situation in his friend's city really casts doubt on the wisdom of his visit.

*Wunjo* expresses the present situation, the wish to reconnect with his friend and share companionship. This causes the sceptic to consider his priorities: does his friendship outweigh his personal safety? And just how unsafe would his trip be in any case? Would this person, his friend, really invite him if the situation was dangerous? Is this just another media exaggeration, with the people in the region simply going about their normal lives without worry?

*Isa* is interesting in the context, since it could be interpreted as two very different results. It represents a force of contraction and isolation. This could be interpreted as going to visit his friend, but keeping his head down when out and about, keeping himself to himself and avoiding the slightest hint of trouble. Or it could be interpreted as withdrawing into himself and staying home, declining his friend's invitation at the present time.

The precise interpretation and ultimate decision would be decided by the personality of the sceptic. But whatever the case, the rune reading has given him scope to examine the question with fresh eyes, revaluating his friendship and the things that are most important to him: loyalty and comradeship, or self-preservation? It also prompts him to check his sources again and perhaps strive to gather more detailed information on what is going on in the region than he has been fed through mainstream media channels. Such a small reading has given him plenty of food for thought, causing him to check his facts thoroughly before rushing to a decision.

This is how divination works. Now this question was pure make believe, I just made it up. It's not a veiled question based on an experience someone I know is having or anything like that, I simply plucked a situation out of the air. The runes selected were purely random, they don't even refer to a genuine person or situation. But look at how apt they are, and how their meanings and principles illuminate the question, causing the fictional querent to examine himself, his motives, his facts and the kind of person he is before making his decision. If three completely different runes had been drawn, they would have given an equally illuminating and informative reading. This is because each rune is an archetypal principle and each in its own way will make us rethink and consider more deeply when drawn in a reading – ***any*** reading – thus inevitably leading to a better considered, wiser decision. So even on this basis, which most 'true believers' would consider heretical and horribly materialistic, the runes become an absolutely invaluable divinatory device, ***providing*** they have been properly internalised and thus enlivened within the psyche first.

By this stage, our sceptic will probably see the sense of also studying the mythology of the North, to add depth and flavour to the runes. He will understand that there is no need to believe in these tales or the beings and characters within them, but that the myths represent a symbolic way of understanding both reality and self.

He may even become so captivated by mythic thinking (which will be discussed in much more detail at the close of this *coagula* section of the book) that he undertakes astral journeys to explore the Nine Worlds of Yggdrasil, understanding these to be representative of the deep places and forces within his own mind, a psychological inheritance from his ancestors. He attributes mythic meaning to his own experiences on these imaginary journeys, but understands their psychological basis.

He is able to accomplish all of this, becoming a skilled magician, without ever once believing in the supernatural. He understands that everything that his magic achieves is through the application of his own mind and Will.

It is a sobering thought that so many cherished beliefs held by so many magicians can be dismissed by this alternative explanation. Because let us reiterate once again, most successful magical Workings require no supernatural agency. What will our sceptic do when he encounters the elusive incidence that does seem preternatural/? We'll look at that eventuality below, but by that time he should be big enough to put matters to the test and form his own opinions.

## The Magic of the Void

The practical methodology known as the Magic of the Void is central to the magical philosophy of The Apophis Club. Before proceeding further, it is necessary to discuss the Magic of the Void here, and its implications given the 'almost entirely non-supernatural' rule established by this current work.

I'm not going to go into detail describing the techniques of the Magic of the Void here, as that is already covered more than adequately by previous Club publications, such as *APOPHIS* and *Draconian Consciousness*. All we need to know at present is that the Magic of the Void works by a process of focusing the attention upon a situation until the metaphorical walls come tumbling down in an ecstatic moment, in which the Void opens within the mind of the magician and his creative power is loosed. It is this which effects the magic.

This is all very well, but what **is** the Void? In previous books, I have sought to answer this question by referring to various mythologies, such as the Norse Ginnungagap, or the Enochian Abyss. But that kind of approach, pertinent as it is in those places, is not going to cut the mustard in a book such as this one, where we are trying to define and discover magic through a non-occult lens.

The Void is potential. It is not things which are, it is things which *might be*. It is common to contrast the Void (the *Nothing* of the title of this book) with the manifest Universe (the *Everything* of the title of this book). It might be more apparent if we reduce the question to a microcosmic level and ask it again from a personal perspective. From a personal frame of reference, the Universe is everything that your senses inform you, it is the objects, people and places that your senses[4] can perceive, and the events and processes that can be perceived occurring – or having occurred – relating to these same things. The Void is the imagination, the things which cannot be measured, which are not tangible, which have no existence except in potential only.

So is the Void real? How can it be if nothing in it actually exists? And yet it is. If I shape a magnificent house in my imagination, adorned with beautifully macabre imagery suitable to my sense of aesthetics, it has no existence. But if I then sketch or paint this house that I have imagined, or write an evocative description of it, its idea becomes at least transmissible to others, through the words and images used. And if an architect then uses this as a basis to draw formal plans of the house, and a firm of builders then construct from those plans, and a team of designers dress the house to match my vision, what was once pure imagination has become solid reality: something has passed from the Void into the Universe, Coming Into Being.

There is a cognate in physics, of course, being the state of the Universe before the Big Bang, before the laws of physics as we know them existed. This primeval, unextended

4 For the purposes of this definition, 'senses' includes those inventions we make to extend our physical senses and investigate things for us, such as microscopes, telescopes, and all manner of other technological information-gatherers.

essence is the abode of the Dragon as understood by The Apophis Club. And the mysterious, dark nothingness of the Void which still enwraps the manifest Cosmos are the wings of that same Dragon, outside of the laws of space-time.

Returning to the microcosmic level to assist our understanding, as these things are easier to grasp on a smaller scale, the Void may be seen as the opening of the subconscious, when the usually hidden parts of the mind offer up their precious creative secrets and abilities. In other words, as we have established, it is that moment at which magic works, when the conscious-subconscious divide is bridged. This is the phenomenon termed the Opening of the Eye in the Void by The Apophis Club, that moment when the magician's encoded communication (his 'spell', such as the runes written in the previous chapter) manage to reach the subconscious, which is able to offer its response, ultimately leading to the successful result. As we have seen, this process accounts for almost all successful magical operations.

But if the Cosmos and the Void share this same relationship, this dance of the Unmanifest and the Manifest, can the same be said of them too? We'll investigate this in the ensuing chapters. First, it is necessary to establish a new perspective upon the Cosmos and the Void, however...

## Never Mind, It Doesn't Matter

Before we proceed any further, we first need to address a possible serious error of understanding. It's another of those 'lies to children', useful models which initially help us to grasp the principles of magic, yet later prove to be troublesome if we assume them to be literally true.

Although at a higher conceptual level, this potential error is in many respects a Remanifestation of that old subjective / objective one that we discussed in the 'Matter and Spirit' chapter of the *solve* part of the book. Although it is a convenient and helpful model to initially assume that the Cosmos and the Void are separate and distinct things, the fact is that they are not. Subjective and objective, in spite of all appearances, are ultimately not irreconcilable; at some level, even your most secret, innermost thoughts exist in the same Reality as the solid foundations of your house. Sure, they're at complete different places on the overall spectrum of Reality, but they are both a part of that spectrum. In a similar way, matter and mind are not opposed; they both have their place on that scale.

You can see where I'm heading here. The Void and the Cosmos are not opposing forces. Not at all. A little thought will show this to be the case. For a start, the two are not equal. Nor is the inequality loaded the way you might think. It would be wrong to say that the Void is immeasurably 'larger' than the Cosmos, because the Void pre-exists the manifest Universe and notions of time and space do not apply to it. It may perhaps be slightly truer to say that the Void possesses more capacity for expression than the Cosmos. After all, the various myriad possibilities and potentials of a thought, idea or event in all of its phases must be far, far greater in scope than the single narrow bandwidth that actualises as a physical event[5]. The Cosmos contains only those things which actually manifest in being, but the Void contains everything which has manifested, will manifest, might manifest, probably won't manifest and will never manifest but exists as a concept anyway. So we are not talking of two equal but opposite things here. We cannot blithely declare that "the Cosmos is the Void, and the Void is the Cosmos", because it simply isn't true, the relative scales are all wrong; indeed the very notion of scale can't possibly exist, due to the nature of the Void[6].

The simple and logical conclusion must be that since the Cosmos is made manifest out of the Void, since its things

---

5 though even this view is challenged and expanded as another 'lie to children' in Apophis Club Lecture #20, 'Time and the World Tree', a philosophical conceptualisation not yet ready for print. Visit the Apophis Club forums at the website listed at the front of this book for further information on subscribing to the lecture series and keeping abreast of the very latest cutting edge ideas in Draconian Magic.

6 It is so difficult to describe these relationships in conventional language, which is why Crowley titled his book devoted to this level of consciousness *The Book of Lies*. Almost everything said is metaphorical. 'The nature of the Void', for instance, is so obviously an oxymoron. But that's all there is to it, so your consciousness will just have to deal with it and make the right calls.

and events are manifestations of one possibility out of the Unmanifest many, the Universe must be considered a part of the Void, a subset in which a plethora of manifest possibilities interweave and cohere in a way that establishes a Universe which exists according to the laws created by the interrelations between its component parts.

You will notice that I have been very careful not to state or imply that the Universe is unreal, nor is it an illusion. It has come into manifestation, it is very real. But ultimately, once its complex, self-replicating pattern fades, it remains a part of the Void in which it formed, upon whose spaceless, timeless surface its patterns played out.

I would bet any money that a lot of people reading this present work have believed up to this point that I was advocating an utterly materialistic view of magic. How very wrong that supposition would be. I am actually saying the Everything (the Cosmos) **is** made from the stuff of Nothing (the Void). So yes, in a sense, I am a materialist, because I see no distinction in essence between these two phases. But if I **am** a materialist by this definition, my 'matter' includes mind stuff and imagination and possibility alongside manifestation. I am the whisper from the Void, tying the Knot of Reality in the Not of potential. Everything is so much vaster than you have ever imagined: it is Nothing indeed.

## In Search of the Miraculous

Throughout this book I have kept reiterating the rule of thumb that almost all successful magical Workings require no supernatural element in order to succeed. I stand by that statement and by the analyses so far given. Some people – particularly those whose need to cast off articles of faith is the greatest – will have been outraged by this statement. Others, either more wise to my ways or simply sufficiently self-aware to think instead of reacting, will have paused and looked at what exactly I have said. These ones may then have asked the question: "Okay, that covers 'almost all' of them, but what about the **others**?"

Now isn't that an interesting question? Does our rule imply that the remaining small incidence of successful magical Workings (i.e. those that achieve their desired result) **do** contain a supernatural element, something that can't be explained by psychology or little understood physical laws, but is unequivocally paranormal?

The answer to this question is: "perhaps". Because it is an answer that requires serious contemplation. Above all, the magician seeks to see Reality as it is, and this demands a measure of truth. The truth in this present case is that our answer cannot be absolute, depending as it does upon subjective interpretation of events.

If you ask me my personal opinion, that opinion would be "Yes, truly inexplicable, miraculous events can and do happen, sometimes spontaneously, but most especially in response to magic." Some examples? How about weather magic? My weather magic is consistently successful. If I want the weather to be a certain way on a certain day, whether fine, still, stormy or whatever, I can more or less guarantee that it will be so. But there can be no physical, causal link between my spell and the weather patterns; if it happens, it must occur as a result of some paranormal process. I have several times successfully predicted winning numbers at roulette and have known with utter certainty when one of these hunches is going to be correct. I have experienced direct clairvoyant sharing of another person's thoughts with such immediacy, detail and clarity that it was undeniable. In a series of experiments run by The Apophis Club a few years ago to develop telekinesis, I experienced a coin moving from its position twice with no physical cause (and no cheating; I was the only person present) and ultimately disappearing altogether. So I have experienced those things that most people would classify as miraculous.

But this is not proof of the type we need in order to answer our question. The weather effects may be pure coincidence; the clairvoyance and prescience may be delusion, or instances of selective memory, shutting out the memory of failures when I had been similarly convinced, but wrong (I have seen such selective memory at work many times with others. I do not believe the cited instances in my own experience to be examples of it, but the possibility cannot be ruled out if we are to be objective). The coin experiment, although satisfying to me, was not carried out under scientifically controlled conditions. I may have imagined it, deluded myself, or I could even be lying about all these things to you. How would you know? Experiments must be repeatable, and no matter how you rate my integrity as a witness, it is not sufficient to take my word for things. After all, I may be wrong and simply deluded even if I am being scrupulously truthful, because the only truth I can share is that which I perceive, which is all well and good unless I have got the wrong end of the stick.

So the further you develop your magical practice and extend your consciousness, the more likely you are to encounter results and experiences which simply don't 'fit the mould', which suggest some kind of intervention in Reality which cannot be explained by conventional means. Indeed, such experiences are not only likely, but inevitable. How you choose to explain them is up to you. You may decide that these startling events are evidence of other dimensions of Reality; or you may simply label them as 'unexplained' and leave it at that, or any number of shades of grey in between. The one thing you will not be able to do is prove that your interpretation is the correct one. All that any of us can do is offer up our own personal 'best guesses' based upon the data so far gathered, for others to consider and accept, reject or adapt as their own experiences lead them. And this is what I have been trying to do with The Apophis Club publications.

You can find my own viewpoint and Teachings, therefore, in the prior publications of The Apophis Club, most especially *APOPHIS*, *Dragonscales* and *Draconian Consciousness*. But I am going to offer the fundamental philosophical basis of that viewpoint in the next paragraph of this chapter, followed by my best possible advice for practical Work in the Concluding paragraph that follows it. Added to which, of course, will be the large number of philosophical questions tackled in the third section of this book.

My personal conviction is that magic absolutely works, and that once a practitioner has discovered its keys, magic works **every time**. Magical change will always follow the path of least resistance when Coming Into Being, and this means that in almost every instance, it will manifest through the psychological and physical laws that have been established to keep our manifest Universe in balance. So if your lust spell is most easily answered by spurring you into plucking up the courage to simply go and talk to the object of your desire, that is how it will happen; he / she will not suddenly be mysteriously compelled to wander over, zombie-like, to submit to your 'indomitable Will'. Ain't gonna happen. But in some cases, only something apparently miraculous will do. I have railed against the idiocy, criminal irresponsibility and sheer fraud of psychic 'healers' and their methods in the *solve* section of this book. All of that I remain adamant about. And yet, on the **very rare** occasion, I have known a magician, feverish with raging determination, apparently pull a loved one back from the very brink of death against apparently impossible odds. But the proviso here is that I have also seen this **fail** to happen on more occasions, and that when it did happen, the level of commitment and applied Desire / fury was incandescent, and that this magician did it themselves. **Not** through any other party, whether God, spirit or so-called 'gifted healer' (a.k.a. stupid twat). So take your lesson from that. As Dr Flowers once put it, any magical result will always be in proportion to the passion and precision of the operator and if you haven't these qualities, you can whistle for it. The essential philosophy underlying these magical 'miracles' as I see them is simply born out of the interrelationship of mind and matter / Void and Cosmos as we have examined them in this section of the book: if the Void can generate and manifest a relatively stable Cosmos within its folds, it surely stands to reason that it can generate and manifest additions / adjustments to that Cosmos also. We'll be discussing / discovering this in more depth in the remaining three chapters of this *coagula* section of the book.

Be that as it may, my advice to new Initiates will always be to put practice before philosophy and to base their ideas and beliefs upon the actual results that they experience, using Occam's razor as their best guideline for interpretation. It is time enough to begin thinking in terms of super-normal explanations when you have had definite experiences to warrant such; then base your philosophy upon your own acquired wisdom and knowledge. Keep your mind open and explanations simple and you will be well prepared for magic.

## CONSCIOUSNESS, ART AND CREATIVITY

In this chapter, we are going to add another element into our reconstruction of magic, one which I have been deliberately dancing around and holding over until it's become somewhat of an elephant in the room. This is the element of consciousness, and the related question of what exactly magic is **for** in any case? Normally, we will be holding such big philosophical questions over till the third part of the book (as we will be doing with the natural extension of this question: what is the Cosmos *itself* for?), but this is one which simply can't be put off and is an essential part of our *coagula* process, our reconstructed magical perspective.

Consciousness is that sense of Self we each possess as a self-aware entity. It is not our thoughts, nor our emotions, these things are its symptoms, not its essence. Consciousness is that which does the thinking and the feeling, which recognises and records and compares these things. Consciousness is not our knowledge or our opinions or our beliefs; it is that which knows and which has access to our knowledge, which formulates our opinions and beliefs based upon what we know and surmise. Consciousness has two defining factors which are extremely important to our understanding of it: consciousness possesses **identity** and consciousness possesses **continuity**.

I'm not going to question the origins of consciousness here, nor debate the limits of consciousness, though both of these questions will be looked at in the third section of the book. For the present, the important thing for us to note is that we are conscious beings. Everything that you tend to refer to as part of "I" is an aspect of this consciousness.

How do we know that we are conscious? Because we know that we are conscious; if we were not, we would not know anything, we would be incapable of knowing or thought.

It is also important to realise that everything we know about ourselves and the world is of necessity filtered through the lens of our own consciousness. When you stop to think about it, it becomes apparent that we can **never** know anything outside of our own consciousness directly; we can only know the impressions, perceptions and ideas that outer things (including other people) make upon our own consciousness. In a very real sense, the world in which we directly live is purely our own consciousness, because all we know of it are its reflections within our own thoughts, those parts of it that can be interpreted and made sense of within our psyches. If I pick up an apple and eat it, I have no direct experience of that apple. I feel and taste only those sense impressions that my brain interprets and filters for me and then passes into my conscious awareness. In many ways, this is indistinguishable from the sense data our minds create and present to us in dreams as we sleep; the only difference is that the (presumed) waking data tends to be more continuously consistent over the perceived passage of time, thus we accord it a greater measure of reality in our worldview and presume these waking experiences to be evidence of a persisting external Cosmos. This is not an unreasonable assumption and is one that I hold to be correct.

But the faculty of dreaming that we have just mentioned is a most curious one. It demonstrates that our consciousness is capable of **independent creation**. It is able to draw together within itself the components of an imaginary world and then to **project itself** – while the conscious mind sleeps – into this imaginary world that it has itself created, and to experience it from a first person point of view, seemingly every bit as solid and real as the reality we experience when awake. Some of the people, places and circumstances in our dreams may be reconstructed from the raw materials of our everyday lives, but other components are created from scratch and may not necessarily follow the rules of the workaday world. We take dreams for granted, but this is an absolutely **astonishing** ability!

It becomes even more astonishing when we learn that according to current psychological knowledge, we are actually dreaming continually, not just when we sleep. It is simply that most of this dream activity takes place in the subconscious mind, at a level too deep for us to be consciously aware of when about our daily business. But nonetheless, we do all have at least some experience of becoming aware of this dreaming whilst still awake. Who hasn't experienced daydreams, becoming lost in reverie whilst listening to some boring lecture or enduring a long train journey? We are still fully awake, but our conscious hold drifts and the *already occurring* dream images rise to the surface, immersing us in their world until something occurs around us which gives us a sufficient jolt to jerk us out of the trance.

But if the subconscious can rise up and take us in daydreams while we are conscious and awake, the reverse can also happen. On occasion, the conscious awareness can surface in the midst of a dream while your body is sleeping. This phenomenon, where you become aware that you are asleep and dreaming whilst still asleep and in the dream world is termed *lucid dreaming*, and developing the faculty is part of the Third Head Work of The Apophis Club. It is a compelling and fascinating experience, and one that is incredibly magically useful. The mind becomes awake within the dream and discovers that the dream world around it is every bit as apparently solid and real as the world it inhabits in waking life. But this dream world can be altered drastically according to Will, because in spite of its apparent solidity, it is made of mind stuff and responds to Will. Initially, lucid dreams tend to be very brief as the shock of finding oneself lucid within the dream state is so startling that you tend to wake up very quickly. But with training and repetition, the state can be prolonged. The implications here just for plain, simple *fun* should be obvious, let alone the magical applications!

This helps to place in context the importance of astral magic, or journeys in the spirit vision. In a sense, it makes absolutely no difference whether these are journeys to 'real' places or not. What matters is that they are coherent, powerful, archetypal experiences which occur when the conscious and subconscious minds connect. They are, if you like, dreams under Will.

But now that we are examining the notion that the Void and the Cosmos are ultimately but one thing, and that mind and matter are one thing, does it really matter if we cannot locate these astral destinations on a map of the conventional Cosmos as understood by geographers and astronomers? Perhaps it is sufficient that we can locate them in our own internal map of the Void. For those who have really absorbed the mythology of their chosen magical tradition, such as our sceptical rune magician of a couple of chapters ago, these astral realms will appear perfectly coherent and will exhibit continuity, conforming to the internal cosmic map of Yggdrasil, the World Tree, complete with its nine distinct worlds and the rainbow bridge of rune paths that run between them. In a sense, this is truly as Real as **anything** gets! Those who insist that an astral location is objectively real and those who counter insist that it is but a subjective notion **both** miss the point, which is the sheer wonder and power and ecstatic majesty of the creative consciousness. This, my friends, is magic!

It seems that consciousness is that place where the Void and the Cosmos meet, where potential passes into manifestation, the creative faculty, the shaping intelligence. Is consciousness the substance of the Void, governing those possibilities which Come Into Being? Is it an interface between possibility and actuality, between Everything and Nothing, or is it the actual stuff of which they are made? Is the entire Cosmos conscious, or is it the product of consciousness, an arena for consciousness to play in? We will be asking some of these questions in the third section of the book and striving to reach an Understanding concerning them. But one thing is for certain from the outset: consciousness appears to be a creator and motivator, not a by-product; it is the organ-grinder, not the monkey.

It is this tremendous creative force within consciousness which gives us one of the clues as to why we Work magic and what magic is ultimately for. It is all about the joy and exuberance of creation and transformation, the bringing into being of new expressions of creative thoughts and ideas. Magic is all about Art, whether that Art be a painting, a sculpture, a piece of theatre, a novel, a poem, a well-cooked meal, a piece of architecture or a fine-tuned engine. Magic – and indeed existence – is all about creative expression and the fascination of stories. When you hear embellishments and shaggy dog stories from such charismatic figures as Crowley, LaVey or Grant, they are being neither liars nor frauds, they are being story tellers and magicians!

MICHAEL KELLY

Do ye likewise!

# The Draconian Gods

Having restored a Vision of the Void and the Cosmos, and the place of magic and our own consciousness within these things, it is now time to turn our attention to one of the mainstays of The Apophis Club curriculum: the Draconian Gods. We need to Understand the place of these archetypal figures in our cosmology.

There are four primary Draconian Gods as defined by the Apophis Work. Some of these can have several aspects and Their names and precise identities will vary depending upon the precise tradition and curriculum followed (for instance, the Lord of Darkness is called upon as Set in the 'vanilla' Apophis curriculum, or Odin in the *Ægishjálmur* variant, or Iaida / Saitan in *The Sevenfold Mystery*. But the primary archetypes are as follows:

<u>The Lord of Darkness</u> – The principle of consciousness itself and the individual Will. The creative impulse, the sense of Self, the ghost in the machine, the rebel against conformity.

<u>The Scarlet Woman</u> – The principle of Desire, pleasure and purpose. The quest for Beauty and the inspiration for immortality.

The Dragon – The timeless, spaceless essence of the Void, which is our ultimate heritage. The sense of continuity and the principle of unbounded imagination and possibility, ever recreating and Remanifesting in new forms.

The Dæmon – The very core of Self, the utmost expression of personal Essence, a projection and aspiration of that which we Desire to Become. The Divine I AM..

It will be seen that each of these four primal Gods is an operant principle in magic. We cannot Work magic without Will; we cannot shape and direct Will without Desire; we cannot conceptualise Desire without Imagination and the awareness of change; we cannot change unless we can appreciate what it is that we are transforming into. So each of these principles is very real and very dynamic and essential to grasp, whether we define them as Gods or not[7]. Therefore, at the very least, to this extent the Draconian Gods are very **real** as practical, operant magical Keys for every member of The Apophis Club.

But are they literally Gods who exist in the ways that the 'man in the street' would understand the term? No, absolutely not, because the 'man in the street' understands very little. The 'man in the street' completely fails to understand **human** consciousness, let alone what we might categorise as Divine consciousness.

So, let's rephrase the question. We know that the Draconian Gods are active, dynamic principles, not static representations of abstracts, otherwise there would be no point in harnessing them in magic. Also, we know they possess consciousness: how could you have such qualities as Will,

7 And one might well argue, what is such a guiding principle, if not a God? And what is a God if not such a guiding principle?

Desire or Imagination without consciousness? So the question can be rephrased as: is the consciousness of the Draconian Gods a manifestation of their own being, or is it a consciousness projected from within the magician?

It's a tricky one to answer, if indeed we can answer it at all instead of simply offering a best current working hypothesis. The Gods as we experience them definitely owe something to ourselves, but they also derive some of their substance / essence from the myths that have grown up around the names and faces they wear in the tradition that we Work within. But since the entire Cosmos manifested out of the Void, not just us, and since consciousness is either the interface or enabler of manifestation (depending upon our interpretation), there is every reason to believe that consciousness will be central to accretions of conscious principles. When you couple this with the hypothesis that mind and matter are actually one and the same thing, and equally 'real', this applies even more so. So if this view of the Universe is correct, the Draconian Gods must possess some kind of Self-consciousness, even if it is of a wholly different nature to our own.

Given that the Cosmos / Void appears to be suffused with consciousness, the most readily acceptable explanation would appear to be to me that the Gods partake of all of these modes of consciousness to at least some extent. They are foci of specific kinds of consciousness, but the origins and manifestations of that consciousness may be multi-faceted. It is worth pausing at this point to consider that exactly the same may be – and probably is – true of human consciousness. For example, the 'you' that other people perceive is not the **real** you who only exists within the event horizon of your own Self; their perception of you is at least as much a product of their own consciousness as it is of yours. Food for thought.

## Mythic Thinking

We have deconstructed magic in the *solve* section of the book, stripping it right back to its bare bones. And now we have gradually applied flesh to those bones once more. Perhaps not the same tired old flesh they once had, but new muscle and sinew, strong to endure. But here at the close of the *coagula* process, there remains one thing left to do, which will serve to get the magical blood pumping once again, giving magic back its heart. This is what I term **mythic thinking**.

Mythic thinking is learning to think in the terms of the magical tradition you have adopted, using its themes and archetypes to define your life, process and transformations. This is **not** the same as religion, it is not a case of 'believing' in Deities, nor is it a case of interpreting symbolic myths as real. It is a matter of understanding that the things that make life matter are the meanings that we attach to it. Mythic thinking occurs when we make our life decisions based upon the principles and codes that matter to us instead of upon pure expediency. It doesn't matter a jot whether these themes and principles matter to anyone else or not; the simple fact that we **choose** to make them matter to us, and that we then act upon them, **makes** them matter.

In the process of living our lives around mythic

principles, we will discover – experientially, not by reading it in a book – what it truly means to be a consciousness acting by Will as an interface between the Void and the manifest Cosmos: we will literally be creating the Universe in our own image as we go. This is easy to say, far harder to truly understand. It can only really by grasped by doing it.

This is why we have gone through this *solve et coagula* process, so that we can Understand and shape the Real. This is something that can never be achieved by those magicians who lurk in the World of Should-Be; in order to effect real change in Reality through consciousness, shaping it to mirror your Desire, you first have to see it as it really Is.

MICHAEL KELLY

# KELLY EXPLAINS EVERYTHING – AND NOTHING

## THE REAL

We have now stripped magic back to its basics, ruthlessly removing multiple layers of belief and supposition, and have then rebuilt it in a robust form, founded firmly upon what we know to be Real.

But what we have discovered is that Reality is a much bigger thing than we had perhaps realised. Even as we removed the notions of such popular occult theories as an 'astral plane', we did not shrink Reality, but rather expanded it, as we were compelled to admit experientially and philosophically the necessity for three separate components which taken together constitute our experience of the Real.

The Material World – This is the world that we can see and touch and experience all around us; the world of manifest things, organised and defined by the laws of physics; the world of the five senses. It is a world of stability, equilibrium and durability, but is still subject to great change and patterns of decay and renewal. The world we share with other living beings.

The Void – The very existence of the material world, and the tendency of things to manifest which did not previously exist, the capacity for consciousness to manipulate and change the material world, all make necessary a potential from which these things arise. A timeless no-place in which everything exists in potential, but nothing exists in actuality. From this the Universe came; to this the Universe will return. In fact, the Universe *remains* within its much vaster (in conceptual, not spatial, terms) folds.

Consciousness – Neither of the two prior states have any meaning without consciousness to perceive and interact with them. Consciousness is the bridge between the two. It is only consciousness that can make sense of purpose of a manifest Cosmos, a stable playground in which to Become. It is consciousness which straddles these two phases of being, conjuring images within the imagination which can then transition into manifestation.

These are the three states of Being (both manifest and unmanifest) that we can be certain of. The lack of any one of these things makes Reality as we know it impossible. It is through the third of these – consciousness – that we can directly experience the other two (consciousness, although manifest in the Cosmos in our flesh and blood, retains awareness of the Void when it looks within and utilises the creative imagination). More importantly, it is through consciousness that the ultimate Draconian God – the Self – Comes Into Being. The Awakened Adept is aware that he manifests his own Self out of the Void at every moment in a series of continual Remanifestations.

It will have struck the astute reader that this model of Reality – a purely experiential model, which is the only model we can truly know – provides a new and dynamic way of considering 'astral' magical operations. In the *solve* part of this book, we set aside the notion that astral planes and so forth were literal, objective 'places', but at the same time, a purely psychological interpretation fails to account for all astral phenomena (although certainly probably accounting for most people's early astral experiences). But now we have another possibility, in which the consciousness of the magician directly taps into the creative Void through the process of mythic thinking and experiences a resonant locality within the imagination; this is fed from the Void, shaped by the symbol-set and myths of the magician's tradition, and may pass certain manifestations through into the material world by an act of Will.

This concept of consciousness drawing upon the Void and feeding into manifestation also gives greater potential depth and meaning to the tools of the magician's tradition. The runes may start out as mnemonic keys, but as Mastery is gained and they penetrate deeper into consciousness, they become living currents, drawing creative potential from the Void, not merely symbols. But all of this, of course, is dependent upon the degree of their absorption into consciousness. A student will use the runes in accordance with the model offered in the 'Runes For Sceptics' chapter in the *coagula* part of the book; it takes a Master to direct the flow of pure Mystery from the Void.

Nevertheless, although this model of Reality requires an advanced degree of Initiation (Fourth Head and higher by the measure of the Apophis curriculum), it remains a useful and informative gauge and aspiration even for those whose Work has not yet reached that level of development.

## What Are the Origins of the Universe?

One of the first philosophical questions that people are moved to ask concerns the origins of the Universe. "Where did it all come from?" Every religion and philosophy from the dawn of time has wondered about this question and offered its perspective. We often scoff at some of these Creation myths now, but this is because modern people have suppressed that important faculty we discussed at the close of the *coagula* section – mythic thinking. A myth of creation is not supposed to be taken literally, it represents a series of progressive manifestations, intended to shed some understanding upon the way things are. We will look at some of these myths later in this chapter. But first, before we can consider the origins of the Universe and the ways in which it manifested, we have to consider another question: what was there **before** the Universe?

Bible believers often get criticised, because when people ask them where the world came from, they get told, "God created it". The sceptic will then reply, "That's all very well, but you're just putting the same question back one step, you're not answering it: where then did God come from?" The same charge can be levelled at many Creation stories, including the scientific notion of the Big Bang; the Big Bang may explain the start of the Universe, but it doesn't explain the primordial, super-compressed matter which actually went bang in order to create the Universe.

The myths are actually surprisingly consistent in their descriptions and nomenclature of the state of things prior to the Creation of the Universe. Norse mythology speaks of Ginnungagap, an expression which is best rendered by a phrase such as 'a magically charged void'. This corresponds with the Draconian conception of the Void which we have already discussed: a Nowhere / Nowhen, with neither time nor dimensions as we understand such things, yet pregnant with possibility. The *Genesis* account in the Old Testament describes the situation prior to the Creation as "without form and void". This description is translated from the Hebrew phrase *tohu wa-bohu*, which is suggestive of such meanings as emptiness, formlessness, confusion, chaos and unreality. This Void, or Abyss, is presumed to be watery in nature (deep, dark, and filled with shifting currents of possibility), as we read of the spirit of God moving upon the face of the waters in the act of Creation. This notion of a primordial, watery Abyss originates in Sumerian mythology, where the Void is the home of a huge Dragon Goddess named Tiamat, who spawns monsters, demons and gods. Tiamat is the first mythic representation of the great Dragon who is the most sacred and supreme Deity of the Draconian current. The Dragon embodies the Void and is all-creation, all-destruction, all-potential.

Every Creation myth then goes on to explain how an enclave of order is established within the chaos of the Void, a world created with proper balance, and with laws to govern it and to ensure its continuance. The Universe is often referred to as "the created order" and this is an apt description, for only order and precise physical laws can ensure the continuance of any creation out of the Void; if it has no rules and mechanisms to bind it together, it will instantly disintegrate back into the charged Nothingness of the Void.

This process of ordering and Creation is often preceded by a great conflict. We can see this in the Sumerian myth, in which Tiamat and Her demons are overthrown and slain by Marduk and the Gods who follow Him; or Ymir is slain by Odin, and the worlds, skies and seas formed from his body, bones and blood. In a similar Greek myth, Cronus separated the sky from the earth, creating the world as we know it, by castrating his father, Uranus. There are two telling facts revealed by a careful study of these myths of primordial conflict: firstly, the new Universe is created from the flesh, bone and blood of the monstrous parent, so the Universe is of the same substance as the Void; secondly, since time does not exist within the Void, the slain parent continues to exist outside of time. Thus, although Tiamat is slain and Her body and blood is used to create the matter of the Cosmos, She still continues to live within the Void.

So who are these Gods who arise in the myths to subjugate the primordial Dragon (or Giant) and shape a coherent Universe from the stuff of Chaos and the Void? They represent consciousness, surely, and it is consciousness that establishes Order upon Chaos, creating an enclosure within which it can exist, express itself and transform.

Of course, since the Universe, for all its Order, must be malleable and capable of change if it is to be a fit place for consciousness to dwell, and since it is in any case ultimately made of the stuff of the Void, it has the seeds of its own dissolution written into it. Every version of the mythic thinking which underlies the Cosmos, foresees an eventual end, whether a Ragnarok, an Apocalypse, or a heat death of the Universe thanks to the Second Law of Thermodynamics. The ordered Universe is but a bubble floating within the limitless, unbounded Void, or a pimple upon its skin. One day (by its reckoning) it will return to the Void (where it has always been, by the Void's reckoning). But we shall return to this. We shall also ask many more questions concerning the purpose and substance of the Universe as we go. But for now, we have witnessed its beginning: the Universe arises as a piece of the Void is ordered and balanced by consciousness, so that consciousness has a place in which to express itself, a magic mirror in which to behold its own face.

It is interesting to note the affinity of the parts of Reality with the Draconian Gods. The Void is the Dragon, whose chaotic nature is tamed and ordered for a span by the Lord of Darkness, the God of consciousness, allowing a beautiful Universe to arise in which He may take His pleasure, represented by the Scarlet Woman. The magician is consciousness clothed in flesh and star-stuff, able to walk in this new realm, to his very great delight.

Play well!

## SELF AND NOT-SELF

We have established the key role of consciousness in the very structure of Reality. It is consciousness that is capable of shaping and limiting the stuff of the Void in order to make a stable enclosure / Universe possible. It is consciousness that is the interface between manifest and unmanifest aspects of Reality, between Void and Cosmos. It is consciousness that knits Reality together.

We ourselves are conscious beings, and it seems likely from the model of Reality we have developed that all things are conscious (though we may not recognise the nature of their consciousness; it may be hugely different to our own), or at the very least all things are *shaped* by consciousness and consciousness remains a causal factor in all things.

So what is it that differentiates our own, individual consciousness from any other consciousness? What is it that makes I, I?

There are several different theories of consciousness, each one generally geared towards the bias of those who promote it. Let's examine a few of the major strands.

There is the theory championed by almost every monotheistic religion[8], in which the individual soul is created

8 You know, the ones descended from that insane fucker, Abraham

by God, but its sense of Self and subsequent wilfulness are inherently sinful. Under this paradigm, it is the duty of every soul to submit itself to God (the originating consciousness) in absolute obedience, or else face being snuffed out or eternally punished.

Then there is the theory prevalent among most other religions and occult schools of thought. In this paradigm, all consciousness is but a part of one consciousness and it is the destiny of all to evolve to the point where we can see our essential oneness and return to a state of pure unity and bliss. This is the basic model of Right-Hand Path thought (as that terms is defined in modern Western schools such as the Temple of Set, I'm not going to get into the nit-picking arguments about the origins of these terms here).

The usual (modern, Western) Left-Hand Path philosophy tends to run along different lines. Each individual consciousness *remains* individual. Different schools teach different origins: some assume that consciousness arises in an individual following birth with no prior existence; others assume it reincarnates, but remains continuous and isolate; others teach that individual consciousness is a spark Gifted by the Lord of Darkness, but is thenceforth unique to its possessor. This consciousness develops and grows and evolves, but remains its own Self. Some schools believe consciousness may be stifled and expire if not properly developed and worked with via Initiation.

The materialistic paradigm holds consciousness to be a by-product of brain activity, a means of species adaptation and survival, with no function other than the purely biological. According to this model, consciousness perishes with the death of the physical body.

Having worked hard to rebuild our Magical Universe after deconstructing it, we need to conceptualise an origin, essence and purpose of individual consciousness which fits with the Reality we perceive and have defined. My current 'best possible model' follows.

We have defined that consciousness is the essential factor to the very existence of an ordered Universe. It is consciousness which shapes the Void in order to create a viable, relatively stable space for existence to unfold, for manifestation to spring forth from the Unmanifest. This First Form of consciousness, who performs the great division and allows Self to arise within a place to Play, we name the Lord of Darkness.

Just as all substance within the Cosmos is ultimately shaped from the stuff of the Void / the flesh of the Dragon, so all consciousness is splintered, or descended (or Gifted, as the term is often used) from the Lord of Darkness. Beings in whom consciousness has developed, establishing a sense of Self, are the Children of Set. The Lord of Darkness is thus the origin of our consciousness.

However, once given, the Gift of Set is established, and the consciousness that grows within us is our own indeed, our own very Self. Just as a spark that jumps from a fire to ignite in a new place will burn on its own, so our consciousness (often called poetically the Black Flame) will blaze with its own glory.

We hypothesise a Universe which is suffused with consciousness, created by consciousness out of the Void as a play arena for consciousness, and our own individual consciousness is a spark from that first consciousness. Given this model, it matters little whether our consciousness first ignites with our own physical birth, developing as our minds are exposed to the stimuli of the world around us, or whether it pre-exists, perhaps migrating from one host body to the next (we will discuss the notion of reincarnation later, so won't pursue this further here). Whatever the case, the source of our consciousness is the consciousness of the Lord of Darkness (whether viewed as a living, Self-aware being[9] or as a nebulous 'field' of consciousness). Once we become Self-aware, our consciousness becomes self-referential and accrues its own nucleus and essence, adding to its Being through Becoming.

In this Draconian model of the Left-Hand Path, as outlined above, the individuated consciousness continues to perpetuate itself, to develop and to grow as its own Self. It remains a spark of the primordial consciousness and has a close affinity to it, even a certain shared / overlapping Essence in those who perform a Priestly function, but it is its own thing and does not 'return' to the originating Flame, though the Lord of Darkness may be 'enhanced' by those sparks that best reflect His Majesty.

From hereon in, the path is ever onward and upward. Perhaps, in far-off times and places, in another cycle of the Void, other sparks may be struck off our own still-burning consciousness, to bring glory and delight to us.

So our consciousness is linked and kindred to every other consciousness, resonant with them, sharing the same source Essence, but it follows its own path, becoming ever more individuated and unique as its Self grows. We are all part of the Cosmos, with our roots in the Void, and our own Self enthroned to appreciate the totality.

So the title to this chapter is ultimately paradoxical. We are our own Selves, individual and apart, distinct from all others, and yet on some level we are linked to all that exists and can enter communion with it. More, through the Void, we are linked with all that does **not** exist, but which has potential and can be imagined by the creative mind.

---

9 which would be suggested by the association with consciousness

## WHY IS THERE EVIL IN THE WORLD?

This is one of the questions that gets posed to every religion or philosophy by sceptics, and it's a good one that requires an answer. “If God is so great and loving, why is there evil in the world? Why is there war? Why do children get sick and die?” These are all valid questions.

The Christian can only answer these questions by vaguely mentioning God's irritating habit of moving in mysterious ways, or referring to a Divine plan, saying that the just will be rewarded and the wicked punished in the end, and besides, people are better off dead and in Heaven with God, aren't they? We should be happy for them, as they've gone to their glory[10]. Some of the grumpier ones may even insist that it's no more than the sick kiddies deserve, since we're all sinners, them included. What was that we were saying about evil in the world? Ah yes, it often wears the good guy badge!

The occultist, on the other hand, will generally mutter something about karma when asked this question. “Oh, karma will sort it all out,” they say, shuffling their feet as they desperately try to change the subject to a more comfortable topic. “Every good deed will be rewarded, every wicked deed punished.” What is it that they're actually saying here? If

10 I've actually heard this said to grieving relatives.

every wicked deed is punished, are they saying that the people suffering and dying now are paying the consequences for being serial killers or whatnot in previous lives? Oh no, try to suggest that line of reasoning and you'll see some very rapid backpedalling as they insist that this wasn't what they meant at all – in which case their precious karma must be selective! Or could it be that what they are **actually** saying when they utter this trite bullshit is simply, "Don't ask me, that's far too hard a question, but I'm a spiritual person, so hey, something spiritual will surely sort it out, because ... well ... it's spiritual, isn't it? In the meantime, I can't deal with this heavy shit."

If that paragraph reads as though I'm sneering as I write it, I am.

For those of you who may still be wondering, there is no karma. It does not exist. Or certainly not in the way that these fools mean. There is only cause and effect, and the patterns of manifestation they create. There is no reward for the meek; there is no punishment for the wicked, except that which might be meted out to them by those outraged by their deeds. There is **NO** cosmic moral compass.

Does our Draconian Magic model have anything to offer in answer to this question? Damn right it does. In order to discover an answer, we must look back once more at the way in which the Universe is created, the stuff it is made of, and the forces that shape it. Then, having found a likely answer, we will be able to basically prove it by looking at a contemporary analogue.

As we have seen, the Universe is shaped out of the Void by the action of consciousness. The fact that the Cosmos is ultimately mind-stuff is illustrated when we look at sub-atomic physics. The deeper we look inside an atom, the more we realise just how much of what we consider to be solid matter is just empty space. And the harder we look at those tiny, charged particles that **do** exist, the less tangible they appear, until finally they seem to represent only a *tendency to exist.* The Universe **seems** so very solid and enduring to us, because that is how our senses have been conditioned to perceive it. In order to enter into the Universe and Play, consciousness must create a totally immersive experience.

Since consciousness is the critical factor in shaping the Universe, it remains a critical factor in its continuance. But consider how many consciousnesses there are, each vying for control, just here on our home planet Earth! So many billions of minds, all tugging their own way, all bleating, "I want! I want! I want!" There are currents and counter currents pulling every which way. Is it any wonder that things break, that disasters happen, that evil deeds are wrought? Because the person committing the evil deed never sees themselves as evil, you know, they invariably think they're perfectly justified. Just take a wander down to your local cheap supermarket, or your Walmart if you're in the U.S.A., and spend time simply observing the people there. Think about the kind of world those people would create if they were in charge. Then get terrified when you realise that they **do** have an equal say in the shaping of the world, and they **are** in charge, or at least as much as any other non-Initiate.[11] **Then** turn round and ask me again why there's evil in the world. Isn't it obvious? All of those small minds and greedy hearts who are only out for themselves, rich and poor alike?

So when people ask you this question, you have an

11 Initiates do have a larger clout, because of the accelerated focus and Understanding of consciousness, allied to Will. But wise Initiates are also aware of the strength of mass movements and the flow of power, which is why they usually harness existing patterns and currents of consciousness instead of swimming directly against the stream.

answer. You can say, "It's got nothing to do with sin or punishment, and it's not something that's deliberately intended either. It's simply the way the world is, because everyone is pulling in so many different directions. The more that people truly want to live in peace, and to cure all disease, the closer we'll move to that reality; it really is that simple. In the meantime, this is the way the world is, and we all must just do the best we can for ourselves and those we love."

Now there will probably be people who object to this perspective, huffing and puffing as they protest, "How dare you, Kelly, you blackguard! If we really had a hand in shaping the nature of the world around us, we would **never** create such a place where suffering and war are so dominant!" Oh yes, you would, you know. Let's just consider the evidence of the worlds we know that we **have** created. I'm talking about virtual worlds in video games. These days, these are so immersive and detailed, many games having 'open world' environments, in which the player can pretty much roam anywhere and do anything. But what kinds of worlds do we place the players in? Without exception, worlds of conflict, worlds in peril, worlds where danger and death lurks around every corner. Why? Because that's what makes it exciting! Even in such games as *The Sims*, players delight in sealing their digital people in rooms without doors, laughing as they piss themselves, panic and finally starve to death. The same is true of the worlds created in other media: in literature, in comics, in art. It is conflict that drives a story, and we are all the heroes of our own stories.

The only difference between a video game world and the 'real' world is that the game world is formed of electrons arranged into patterns by lines of code. This is then **presented** to the player as a coherent, three-dimensional environment which he can interact with through the screen and controller. But hold on … go back and reread the paragraph which starts at the foot of page 135 and finishes at the top of page 136, commencing with " As we have seen, the Universe is shaped out of the Void..." and finishing with "...consciousness must create a totally immersive experience." Doesn't this just say **exactly** the same thing about the Universe as I've just said about a computer simulated reality?

The Universe really is an exciting game that our consciousness projects itself into. Remembering that this is so can help us deal with the parts which are misery and suffering, recognising that yes, this is **precisely** the kind of world we would expect people like humanity to create! There is a comfort in knowing that illness, hardship and suffering are not planned and that we can make a difference by combating greed and indolence, which create these things as their by-products.

## WHERE DO WE GO WHEN WE DIE?

Here's another question that everyone wants to know. The fear of death is deeply ingrained within us. The sense of Self is so pervasive that it cannot conceive of the possibility that it might cease to exist. Yet we know that the body wears out and perishes. So what is to become of us?

Various religions and philosophies have proposed various different answers to this question, sometimes to soothe the worries of their adherents, sometimes to propose genuinely held and deeply considered thoughts, sometimes to terrify their adherents into obedience and submission. Let's examine some of these before we propose a Draconian answer:

The creeds devolved from that ancient psychopath Abraham[12] revolve around reward or punishment of the deceased by a clearly insane and sadistic God. The faithful are promised eternal bliss in the presence of the Almighty; the wicked (or even those good, honest people who dared to believe in the wrong thing) are punished eternally by being cast into Hell, generally visualised as a Lake of Fire, beside

12 or at least Christianity and Islam, less so Judaism, which is much less vocal about post-mortem matters and does not promise an afterlife specifically.

which the faithful may pleasantly picnic while they enjoy the screams of the damned.

Needless to say, this belief, conceived purely to suppress and enslave, is rejected outright as pure and utter garbage[13]. Since we are each an individual consciousness, the only Hell is that which an individual may create for themselves, due to their own guilty conscience, lasting only as long as their masochism may continue. There is no God who sits in judgement and decrees our fate.

Materialistic science, holding the mind and consciousness to be but a by-product of brain activity, naturally holds that the only place we go when we die is into a grave or a cremation furnace. The mind, the sense of Self, the personal consciousness, all are snuffed out. There are magicians who also hold this view, believing that life is a wonderful and magical phenomenon, but that it ceases (on a personal level) with the death of its physical vehicle. This opinion is a lot more rational than that offered by most religionists, but it does not fit with the model of Void, consciousness and Universe that we have discovered, a model in which consciousness is the originator, not the product[14].

Other religions – and most New Agers – hold that we reincarnate. When our body dies, the soul vacates it, and after a greater or lesser period of time, is reborn in a new body, to live a new life. This idea is common amongst Hindus, Buddhists and also features heavily in the original European beliefs, being referenced in ancient Greek literature, and with stories of the rebirth of dead heroes also occurring in the Celtic and (to a lesser extent) Norse sagas. So this belief is a very old and very deep and very pervasive one, possibly the

---

13 However, do see the final chapter later, 'What Ifs?', for some further speculation and debate.

14 Nevertheless, I will refer you once again to the 'What Ifs?' chapter for further discussion of this theme.

most common of all 'after death' scenarios, apparently not shared by only the three detestable Abrahamic abominations, the monotheistic religions of Christianity, Islam and Judaism.

In some systems, such as the Hindu. Buddhist and Greek, there is a moralistic bias to reincarnation, as the next life and its circumstances are determined by the manner in which the previous life was lived; criminals, cowards and the dissolute finding themselves in much reduced circumstances the next time around. In other cases, such as the Celtic, this element is absent and rebirth occurs purely through a person's great vitality and vigour of Self. Those with mighty spirits arise in might again; the weak and unassuming must strive anew to better themselves. Also, in some of the belief systems, a person may be reborn in any culture, or indeed regress to an animal form if they lack worth. But in the Celtic and Norse strands, rebirth is always among the same culture and very often the same family line or close genetic pool.

I find the Celtic ideal of rebirth far more convincing and rational than the other notions of reincarnation, and we will return to discuss this more thoroughly in the next chapter. But for the purposes of this current chapter, I am going to reject reincarnation as a complete explanation for what happens to us when we die. As we will discuss in the next chapter, there may well be a rebirth mechanism at work, but it is not by any means a whole and complete answer. To find this, we must look again at the implications of our Draconian model of Reality.

Let's ask our question again and think about it: "Where do we go when we die?" The answer can only be, "Nowhere." And I mean this quite literally: Nowhere is the Void, our point of origin, before we came into manifestation. The Void is timeless too, it is Nowhere / Nowhen. We have always been there. I am there now as I am typing this; you are there now as you are reading this, because now is the only time that exists there. So quite literally, we go Nowhere when we die.

But this explanation works on more than one level, depending upon the emphasis with which you phrase it. We 'go Nowhere' as a reference to the Void, but it also means that quite literally we don't go anywhere. Why? Because we are already there. Our consciousness is already rooted in the Void, it always has been and it always will be; there is no need for it to go anywhere, because it is already there. When our physical body dies, our consciousness withdraws from it, but it is already in the Void and has been all along, as witnessed by the way in which it can use creative imagination and employ abstract thinking, the mind wandering into realms of its own creation even whilst in the flesh. So according to this model, you don't need to worry about the demise of your physical body, because it is only the projected focus of your consciousness that is moored there; your Essence is still in its timeless Everywhere / Everywhen / Nowhere / Nowhen, where it has always been. You don't need to worry about immortality, because you're already alive and immortal now (if immortality has any relevance to a Self that is ultimately timeless). In other words, and returning to our previous analogy of the Universe being like a video game, death is similar to the player logging out of the game and returning to his larger life outside it. When we die, we 'log out', but we have only put down the controller and returned to a larger perspective.

Several of the psychological models developed by Initiates of some of the traditional Mystery schools (such as Egyptian, Norse and Celtic) are very complex and intriguing, suggesting that parts of our awareness and experiences remain accessible at certain levels within the Universe, such as in Hel or Asgard in Norse tradition, plus a shade which may be reached / communicated with by relatives or magicians.

These may be interpreted also by such oft-used phrases as 'collective unconscious', 'inherited memory' or 'atavistic memory'. In any case, there is a good argument that some aspects of the life we have just led may remain accessible to the consciousness of others, or to our new manifestations if we are indeed reborn. Some of these soul models may be studied in earlier publications of The Apophis Club, most particularly *APOPHIS* and *Ægishjálmur*. But they are incidental to our main realisation here: that the Essential Self is timeless and does not need to 'go' anywhere when the body dies, because it is already beyond the body.

## Do We Reincarnate?

Continuing the argument of the previous chapter, we have concluded that according to the Draconian model of Reality, the Essential Self, the consciousness that is the true 'I', is established between the two poles of the Void and the Cosmos, above and beyond both, and thus outside the confines of the body alone. Thus, it need not 'go' anywhere when the body dies, because it is already in its proper place, the body-fixated awareness being but an extrusion, a projection of its real Being.

We did not rule out the possibility of reincarnation in that discussion, but set it temporarily aside since it was not central to our study and realisation of the nature of the Essential Self and its continuity. But it will be interesting to return to this question now, and ask ourselves, “So, **do** we reincarnate?”

Many occultists believe so, and many – including several that I have the utmost respect and admiration for – can give detailed accounts of past life memories. Students of the methods of Aleister Crowley will be aware of at least two practices he taught with a view to accessing the memories of previous lives, and Crowley himself claimed a long list of prior incarnations[15]. But respect and admiration do not constitute proof. We need to analyse such claims rationally, allow for wish fulfilment (see the footnote 15 below!) and carefully examine the case and precedent for reincarnation.

There are certain phenomena in nature which suggest that a kind of reincarnation would be a perfectly natural – perhaps even an expected – process. After all, everything else in nature recycles, springing up, fading away, only to recur in new forms. Even things that pass away and disappear don't **actually** disappear. The elements they were composed of are reconstituted in one way or another.

We're not only talking about physical things either. Einstein tipped us off that energy can neither be created nor destroyed, it can only change its state.

So if this is true of matter and energy, why would mind-stuff be the only thing that it was **not** true of? That would simply not make sense. So there is a certain rational precedent for assuming that thought patterns, ideas and personality traits will recur.

There is also a magical Law to describe this process, which is summed up in the Word **Remanifest**, the Law of Magus James Lewis. This is the Understanding that the magical patterns we create within ourselves and define ourselves with continue to self-replicate and will inevitably Remanifest, bringing us back into being. Remanifestation is discussed in some of the earlier Apophis Club volumes, also in the third volume of my autobiography, *The Children of Set*.

Now we come to the tricky bit, because there may actually be more than one mechanism at work here. You see,

---

15 Rather hilariously, if we listen to the exaggerated claims and oneupmanship bids of some of his followers, he himself would appear to have been reincarnated at least a hundred different times simultaneously since his death, with each 'incarnation' possessing a bare hundredth of his genius!

your thoughts, memories and emotions are not you. They are manifestations of you, they are expressions of you, they are projections of your Essence, but they are not actually you. They are, if you like, the symptoms of your existence, the ripples created by the movement of your consciousness. But the true you is your consciousness itself, not its extensions or accretions. Your thoughts, memories and emotions are ripples created in the Universe by your interactions with it, but your root consciousness has its origins in the Void and is an interface between Void and Cosmos: it is **not** just a part of the Cosmos, whereas its thoughts, memories and emotions are. This is a very important distinction, which will add a layer of complexity to our conclusions that very few ever stop to consider.

Let's leave aside the thoughts. emotions, and so forth for the moment. We will come back to them as they're an important consideration, but first we need to concentrate on the most important things: that spark of unique consciousness which is truly you.

For a start, we can rule out those moralising, karma-riddled doctrines which characterise much thought of reincarnation. Your consciousness enters into manifestation in order to Play, seeking its own reflection in the ever-shifting kaleidoscope of Reality. Incarnation is a joyous choice, a player immersing in a game, not a tedious chore of sin and punishment.

From what we know of magic, consciousness and Reality, it seems apparent that consciousness desires to enter the material world and experience it. This is the very reason for which a stable Universe has been created from the Void. The incarnation of consciousness is therefore a willed choice, not some sort of karmic bondage. If we hold this to be true, then it is only logical to assume that after experiencing one incarnate life, consciousness will desire to experience more.

After all, it hasn't yet seen and experienced everything in that wonderful, immersive manner which is Life. We can therefore assume that reincarnation of the Essential Self occurs along the lines of the Celtic model proposed earlier, i.e. it is a resultant of the intense vitality of the heroic soul, eager to play the game again, not a reward or punishment. Incarnation is a Willed act. This realisation points us to another conclusion: if incarnation is a Willed act, it is something which **may** occur, depending upon the Will. It is not inevitable, it is not automatic, it is a choice. We will explore alternative notions of post-mortem existence in the next chapter.

When an individual incarnates, who do they become? In most cases, no one special. They are just one more person on an over-populated planet (there may be other planets with life, of course, but we'll simply set that speculation aside as a possibility and outside of our current knowledge and experience). If we use that video game analogy once again (because it really is a remarkably pertinent one), they are level 1 characters, with no special abilities or characteristics, just starting out in the game. And most subsequent lives will be similar, while the 'player' continues to accrue needed experience to develop their character. It's probable, therefore, that they may pop up in a different place and a different culture each time, as they learn the ropes.

What happens when someone becomes an Initiate[16]? An Initiate is someone who has seen beneath the surface of the world in which he / she is manifest, someone who has

16 Note that in this instance, I use the term Initiate to denote anyone who has been touched by the Mysteries, not just formal magicians or mystics, but boundary-leaping scientists, artists, writers: those in whom the creative Will and Imagination are strong. Einstein and Pratchett were more Adept than most Hierophants.

glimpsed the workings of the machine and has intuited the Void which lies beyond it. In other words, this is someone who has remembered his / her true identity and source whilst in the flesh. Given this Understanding of the Universe and the Self, this person may now begin to develop and accrue greater skills and insights, a real sense of purpose and a passion to achieve. True magicians may tap back into the Void and become able to use the programmer's skills and cheat codes whilst still immersed in the game, in order to accelerate their learning and Becoming. To again use video game language, this Initiate then reaches a point where upon physical death, they have reached a stage where it has become worthwhile to 'save their game', so that they may resume more or less where they left off.

This is where we get back to the mind-stuff we mentioned earlier: the thoughts, memories and emotions and skills, all the knowledge and wisdom accrued during life which is not part of the Essential Self, the core consciousness. In most cases, this is all small stuff of no consequence. In a couple of generations' time, no one wants or needs to remember how you accidentally sat on your Aunt Mabel's best hat, or how bored you were while stock checking at work last Tuesday. And even the greater, peak achievements are small stuff when placed in context. Nevertheless, these things remain in the sea of consciousness surrounding the world, helping to shape new generations from those who have gone before, all leading to the ultimate evolution of mankind and the enhancement of all our experience and knowledge.

We spoke earlier of the various parts of the soul, and the various worlds, as defined in many magical psychological and cosmological models. Much of this everyday accretion of humdrum affairs will likely never be needed again, at least not in detail. It sinks down to Hel to rest in deep slumber, capable of revivification if strictly necessary, but dormant. The peak experiences and ground-breaking insights ascend to Asgard, becoming accessible to the Deific, shaping consciousness of our race, increasing our collective wisdom and potential all the while. The personality that we wore whilst in the now deceased life abides for a while as a shade, lurking in the hearts and memories of those who knew us. This shade is what may be evoked in necromancy, a shadow of memories of what the person once was. The conscious, Essential Self is **never** evoked through necromantic magic, only the cast-off, timebound personality shell[17].

But let's get back to the Initiate. The purpose and function of Initiation (whether consciously realised or not) is Self-integration and personal evolution. The Initiate gains wisdom and magical power by bringing all the parts of his being into harmonious balance, all working towards a single end. This creates a very different situation upon the death of the physical body.

Because the Initiate has integrated the various aspects of his manifest self into his Essential Self, and has gained considerable insight, skill and power in consequence, this integration does not simply decay upon death, with all of these attributes fluttering off into the collective unconscious. Instead, the Initiate may retain those parts and skills and insights which are useful, carrying them forward into another life, thus gaining a considerable head start and having a host of learned abilities available from the outset. This is that 'game save' scenario I mentioned earlier, and accounts for the truly gifted people active in the world.

So, the Initiate is one who begins to carry increasing memories, skills and knowledge from one life to the next, as he / she becomes increasingly evolved and integrated.

---

17 You may read of my own necromantic experiments in the Apophis Club titles *Gods and Monsters* and *The Sevenfold Mystery*.

However, this makes the choice of vehicle for reincarnation by necessity a much less random prospect. The Initiate will now seek out a host body which has a strong resonance with what he / she has been before, to ensure a good 'fit' of attributes and a smooth path to reintegration and continuation of his / her Work. This implies that the Initiate will seek rebirth within the same culture – and where possible, the exact same family – as previously.

This is borne out by many of the European mythic traditions, such as the Celtic and the Norse, in which heroes are seen to be reborn within the same tribe / clan, often to their own children or grandchildren[18]. When speaking of this conscious, Initiated process – that sought after by magicians – I use the term 'rebirth' in preference to reincarnation.

One further factor remains to be mentioned, which further distinguishes the rebirth of the Initiate from popular ideas of reincarnation: in the Celtic tales, there is more than one instance in which the same individual is incarnated in more than one person at the same time! A hero reborn in his own son, for example, who lives alongside his father and rises to full ascension following his father's death. The spark of consciousness is not as restricted as we like to think it is and may inhabit two minds at once. Renowned Thelemic magician Lon Milo DuQuette wrote a song about reincarnation titled *The Hero of Megiddo*, in which he refers to having once been triplets, wryly commenting "Not sure how that works!" Give it some thought!

18 The Celtic doctrine of rebirth is referenced in my *Book of Ogham*, and my biography of English shaman Dusty Miller 13th is also worth reading in this respect: *WyrdWood: The Story of Dusty Miller*.

## WHAT IS THE DISCARNATE STATE LIKE?

I stated in the previous chapter that rebirth is a willed choice, being neither inevitable nor automatic. This must lead us to wonder what the state of our consciousness must be like when it is **not** clothed in a physical body?

For a start, we can safely assume that it will no longer be encumbered by the things that often seemed so important whilst in the body. Love and Desire are great motivating forces for the Self and these mighty engines will no doubt continue to drive us, but we can forget about all the petty emotions and concerns that bother us in our everyday lives. All of the little jealousies and biases and lusts and cravings, all of those programmed reactions which arise out of biological chemicals or learned responses instead of pure Vision – none of these things will be of the slightest relevance to the consciousness devoid of a body.

One thing we can be certain of is that the way we think in a discarnate state will be very different from the way we think whilst in the flesh. For a start, we will have no senses, these are all physical contrivances to enable us to interact with the physical world. Reality itself, let alone the way in which we perceive it, would be radically different. There really is no way of conceiving the difference between incarnate consciousness and discarnate consciousness, and when discussing such subjects as “life after death”, this is a fact which almost everybody completely fails to grasp. Nevertheless, if our Draconian model of Reality is correct, then such a state of consciousness necessarily exists, since that is our point of origin. But the only way to even begin to conceptualise it – and this is a thing that we **should** meditatively attempt, at least those of us who have progressed to Fifth Head level and beyond – is to begin by stripping away all those thoughts, ideas and impressions that it most definitely is **not** and then see what remains!

Of course, the fact that a consciousness is discarnate does not mean that it has left the comforting confines of the Universe. This is why every magical tradition establishes a number of worlds at varying 'levels' of the Cosmos. These worlds may be visited and defined by the incarnate magician through so-called 'astral' Work as defined previously, and may prove to be aspects of the Universe in which discarnate souls may act or abide for greater or lesser periods. Thus, a soul may ascend to Asgard or travel the Celtic Land of the Ever-Young. It takes a truly Draconian consciousness to wish to dip toes directly in the Void. But it seems likely that even those souls which are reborn will spend a certain time discarnate and recovering their bearings / sense of True Self.

The thing that seems obvious to me, however, and which runs completely contrary to the expectations of most 'spiritual' people and traditions (except the Norse, in which it is quite apparent, and also the Satanic), is that the Universe was created deliberately, as a playground. This is the place where we are **supposed** to be. It was our Will to become manifest, physical beings, and this is the world in which our joy is wrought. So rebirth and the Remanifestation of Self in the physical arena is the right and proper goal of the Initiate.

## WHAT IS THE MEANING OF LIFE?

This is the **big** question of course, the one which every religion and philosophy attempts to answer. What is all of this actually **for**? All manner of soul-searching, agonising and moralising has been expended over the centuries and dumped unceremoniously upon our heads in response to this question. Most of it has been way off the mark, and all of it has served to only muddy the waters. The answer is absurdly simple and recursive and I give it here before explaining it:

**The meaning of life is to discover – or create – the meaning of life.** There now, wasn't that easy?

The reasoning behind this answer is implied in every chapter of this section of the book so far. The Universe is established by consciousness acting upon the Void, the purpose of that action and creation being to establish a relatively fixed and coherent arena which consciousness can enter in order to explore its own Being. The reason that primordial consciousness – that which we name the Lord of Darkness – sparks off new minds and sees new consciousnesses arise, is so that it has other minds to give input into the Universe, shaping it in unforeseen ways, so that it will be a real adventure, not the stale product of a single awareness alone. Each consciousness measures itself against and to some degree sees itself reflected in, the other consciousnesses it discovers. Every entry into the manifest world is new and original. because it is shaped by other centres of consciousness as well as our own. The whole thing is a wonderful game, a great diversion, a process of Self-discovery. Everything is Play.

It is through this process of immersion in the world and living within it that Being can experience the more active and expansive state of Becoming.

## What is the Abyss?

There are two major magical Workings and realisations within the path of every Initiate. These were first clearly defined by Aleister Crowley, who described them as the attainment of the Knowledge and Conversation of the Holy Guardian Angel, and the Ordeal of the Abyss. The Apophis Club concurs that these two events are the major focal points of Initiation.

In his early writings, based around the Qabalistic model of the Hermetic Order of the Golden Dawn, Crowley describes the Holy Guardian Angel operation as coming first, being centred in the Qabalistic Sephirah of Tiphareth. Later, when invoking the Enochian Æthyrs, he would reverse this order, discerning that the Abyss is faced in the Tenth Æthyr, ZAX, whilst the full experience of the Holy Guardian Angel is not attained until the Eighth Æthyr, ZID. This latter ordering is also the doctrine of The Apophis Club, in which the Abyss experience occurs during the arising of the Fourth Head, as the Eye Opens in the Void, and the Dæmon is comprehended and indwells during the arising of the Fifth Head. Although the matter is not absolutely critical and all such curricula are by definition artificial segmentations of complex processes: any magician capable of Opening the Eye in the Void will inevitably have at least *some* Understanding of the Dæmon, and vice versa. But the Void / Abyss followed by the Dæmon / Holy Guardian Angel appears the most cohesive and satisfactory process. We will therefore hold over discussion of the Holy Guardian Angel till the next chapter and deal with the Abyss first.

There are all manner of contradictory and wholly unsatisfactory explanations of what the Abyss is, which is not surprising since it is Not. The Abyss is described as the brink between Creation and the Unmanifest; it is guarded by a terrible Archdemon named Choronzon; it is a place of Chaos, confusion and dissolution, in which every thing that is is also its own opposite. It is said that the ego cannot survive there and would be torn to pieces by the contending forces.

It will be blatantly obvious to anyone who has read even a fraction of Apophis Club magical literature that the Abyss is in fact the Void: the Creative potential out of which the Universe was spawned, through the action of consciousness.

So what does this imply about the Abyss experience? It means that the Initiate who has advanced to this stage has experienced anew the underlying structure of Reality, having recognised the Void as the Nothing which lies behind Everything, with consciousness – in this case, his / her **own** consciousness – as the interface between the Manifest and the Unmanifest.

Note that I stress this as the Abyss **experience**. It is not an intellectual knowledge; it is not a belief; it is not a 'grasp of the fundamentals'; it is a full on, world-shattering **experience**, capable of breaking the sanity of the unprepared. No amount of book learning or meditation can prepare the psyche for the realisation of its own phantasmal nebulosity in the face of the immensity of the Void, when it seems in that crushing moment of apprehension that Everything will be swallowed up in Nothing. It is an extreme, peak experience that changes your life irrevocably. If you have felt it, you will know it; if you haven't, don't kid yourself and don't try to kid others, because it stands out a mile.

This Abyss experience is the focal Initiation of The Apophis Club, when the Fourth Head of the Dragon – that of the Serpent itself – rises into consciousness. In that moment, the mind of the magician passes beyond the bounds of the Universe and touches the creative potential of the Void, capable of manipulating all of the possibilities that may be found in that Neverplace / Neverwhen.

It will be Understood that the term 'crossing the Abyss' is a misnomer, another of those 'lies to children' to help them picture the inconceivable in their minds. There is no 'other side' of the Abyss to cross over to, there is only the plunge into Infinite Nothing, the Neverness of Ginnungagap, filled only with the magical charge of possibility.

Nor can consciousness remain within the Void. How could it, for there is Nowhere for it to remain? With its first thought, it triggers fresh creation and hurls itself back into the Universe, the arena which consciousness has created to express itself through. Whether the Abyss experience is subjectively seconds or centuries, its objective reality is a single moment only, before Remanifestation necessarily occurs. The longer the consciousness can endure as a mere observer, without a single thought, the more of the Void it may perceive in its lightning flash revelation. But as soon as a fresh thought intrudes, the experience is over and consciousness Remanifests in its former place. But when it does so, it is very much changed.

This Remanifested consciousness, which brings back experiential awareness of the Void within itself, is what constitutes what is misguidedly termed the 'other side' of the Abyss. The so-called Supernal Sephiroth of the Qabalah, or the innermost nine Æthyrs of the Enochian system, are metaphors for the Void-transformed consciousness of the magician. These 'supernal' realms are within our own Selves, now able to bridge Reality and draw new stuff through from the Void at Will. The Initiate becomes a Master, who changes a situation simply by being present within it, a conduit for all possibility.

I am not lying when I say that this experience transforms the world and the Initiate. There is no return from it. And it is a source of constant irritation to hear people talking of such things who have no experience of it. It's like listening to a precocious schoolboy, who's never even had an erection, bragging to his friends, trying to convince them he's had sex.

Don't cheapen the experience of the Abyss through bragging or lies. It is actually the most simple thing imaginable, as all truths are, but it shatters worlds and should not be sought unless you are willing to be completely changed, with no way back. You will know them by the starlight in their eyes and the lilt in their voices.

## WHAT IS THE HOLY GUARDIAN ANGEL?

The term Holy Guardian Angel was derived from the *Abra-Melin* grimoire and adopted by Aleister Crowley in his curriculum of Work for his A.'.A.'. Order. To gain the 'Knowledge and Conversation of the Holy Guardian Angel' is a magical operation to connect the magician to his / her personal tutelary spirit. Some people interpret this to be a being distinct from the magician's own Self, others hold it to be a manifestation of the magician's Higher Self. It is my firm conviction that the Holy Guardian Angel phenomenon – whilst perfectly capable of promoting an alternative and more advanced perspective – is most definitely a projection from the most Initiated part of the magician's own Self.

In Apophis Club nomenclature, this entity is most often referred to as 'the Dæmon'.

We have dealt with the various ill-considered thoughts and theories concerning 'Higher Self' entities in the *solve* part of the book, so some readers may be bemused to find the concept reintroduced here. But the simple fact is that it can be a very useful exercise when trying to gain insight and deal with a problem to perform an invocation which coalesces a coherent and communicative projection of the most initiatorily advanced and focused aspect of your Self, cutting through all the fog, distractions and illusions to reveal truth with the utmost clarity.

This perspective, when the Flame of consciousness burns brightly like a star, dispelling all illusions and smoke and mirrors, comes naturally to those who have already passed through the experience of the Abyss, having Opened the Eye in the Void. To commune with the Dæmon is to invoke the timeless, all-seeing perspective of that Eye whilst still grounded here on Earth. This is why The Apophis Club concurs with Crowley's later placing of the Knowledge and Conversation of the Holy Guardian Angel at a point beyond the Abyss, in ZID, the Eighth Æthyr. In the Apophis Curriculum, the Opening of the Eye in the Void is the peak experience of the Fourth Head, with Knowledge and Conversation of the Dæmon following as part of the Fifth Head Work.

Nevertheless, most magicians earnestly involved in Third Head, or even Second Head, Work within the Apophis curriculum, should be able to at least connect with their Dæmon to some extent in order to streamline and empower their magical Path.

## If You're Such a Great Magician, Why Aren't You a Millionaire?

Now this is a great question, and one which is often asked! In fact, it was posed to me in a comment on one of my Youtube videos just a few weeks ago, so I'll begin by providing my answer from there, and will subsequently expand upon it. After all, it's not enough to talk the talk if you're not seen to walk the walk.

The Youtube video in question is one in which I demonstrate the Pharaoh posture, also known as the God posture, one of the basic pieces of posture work described in *APOPHIS*. It can be viewed at the following URL:

**https://www.youtube.com/watch?v=_P2h6wM_w0k**

Viewer Tina Sizemore commented upon the video as follows:

*"if this works why are you not winning at life? i need to get ahold of Charlie Sheen and see what poses that Olde Warlock is using."* [sic]

I replied as follows:

*"+Tina Sizemore Lol, I'm doing very well, thank you, married to the woman I want to be with, living in the country house I've always wanted with a spectacular view and in the process of withdrawing from the rat race.*

*"You get you what you put in, magic isn't an easy route, you don't just wave a wand and become a millionaire. But you can definitely shape yourself into the person you want to be and live the life you want to live. But it takes work, even with magic. Nothing is for nothing.*

*"But if you're asking me if I'm winning at life? Absolutely! This works, but I've never promised it's easy. Magic is bloody hard work, because it requires real change and commitment, it will take you to pieces before putting you together again and the You who succeeds won't be the same you as now."*

That reply was a pretty good summary, actually. If you want to use magic to acquire riches, you can certainly do so. But you can't expect to draw one sigil, or burn one candle, or summon one Demon, and suddenly there'll be money sprouting out of your ears. Magic can – and does – work wonders. But the simple formula is that the amount of Work you put into it is in direct proportion to the results you get out of it. If you want to use magic to bring you riches, you'll have to work at it body and soul. You'll get there, but you'll need to be obsessed with getting there.

And that's the whole problem, you see. Because if you're obsessed with getting rich and are spending every moment either conjuring for money, or going out into the world to put your plans of wealth into action, you're going to have no time for anything else. And those who practise magic for any length of time quickly come to discover that nothing is so rewarding as working to transform themselves.

There are many reasons why most magicians aren't

rich[19], and a lot seem to be permanently strapped for cash. Magic is an expensive hobby if you're really going to give it your all. Many of the books we chase after and read are very costly. (Mine aren't, but that's my deliberate choice, and not all occult authors follow my lead.) Magicians know the value of the Creative Imagination and thus are great art lovers, with a tremendous sense of aesthetics. The works of art with which we surround and enrich ourselves are not cheap. The more initiated the magician, the greater their appreciation and quest for Beauty. Magicians also tend to travel much more widely than most people, always on a pilgrimage or quest to some place or purpose. Travel does not come cheap.

So a magician worth his / her salt will have an enormous drain upon his / her finances as a matter of course. No matter how much money comes in, more is always needed. But then, the magician truly understands money to be but an illusion, a means of exchange, not a thing in itself.

Most established magicians are actually pretty comfortable, bringing in ample money, even if it's nearly always instantly spent. But they use their magic to live where and how they want, to surround themselves with the artistic and aesthetic environment that they desire. Most magicians who apply themselves also manage to arrange their working lives to reflect their inner selves, either finding employment that really suits them and which they enjoy, or gradually finding the means to become self-employed or financially independent. Such changes can take a few years to fully effect, but the magician who sets their mind upon these goals will succeed.

But truly **rich** magicians? Magical millionaires? As I've said, it's not impossible, but it's not likely, simply because most magicians have things to do and to focus upon which are far, far more important to them than the mere acquisition of

19 Some are, don't doubt that.

money. They may conjure cash to see them through immediate cashflow shortages[20], but most of the time they'd rather be focusing upon more interesting matters.

20 and in such cases, the Will responds quickly and provides the necessary funds, because it is responding to genuine, deep level Need, not greed or mere wanting.

## How Can We Aspire to be Gods in Such a Vast Universe?

It's a common feeling to look up into the night sky and see the vast sweep of stars overhead and to realise that these are all suns, inconceivable distances away, so far in fact that it has taken the light from some of them many hundreds of years to reach us, so that we are even looking backwards in time as we stare out into space. Then we learn that the stars that we can see with the naked eye are only the tip of the iceberg, that the Cosmos stretches on into near infinity. There are photographs taken by some of the world's most powerful telescopes which show incredibly coloured and beautiful nebulae and gas clouds which span absolutely incredible distances, far larger than our minds can even begin to conceptualise. In those rare moments when we do perhaps begin to realise just how large these things are in comparison to our own little world, it is literally mind boggling. Our poor brains simply cannot take it and either shut down momentarily or shrink from the the thought. We just cannot deal with such overpowering immensity. The Universe is like a great, gargantuan monster, just waiting to swallow us whole (perhaps literally, if we listen to those theories of super massive black holes).

It is a well-worn saying of the Left-Hand Path that we

aspire to be Gods. This is something reflected in the very first promise spoken to Eve by the Serpent, that “ye shall become as Gods, knowing good and evil”. But when the sense of the immensity of the Universe grips us (let alone the realisation that the manifest Cosmos is but one possible expression of the immeasurably vaster possibilities within the Void), we can only cower and bleat, “But how can we possibly call ourselves Gods in the face of this, against which we are so insignificant, such tiny specks, who cannot even measure the Universe in our minds without risking madness?”

There are actually two answers to this question, looking at it in two distinct and different ways. The first response is to say that most people (including many of those strutting their stuff on the Left-Hand Path, usually the same ones who consider themselves the 'coolest') have completely the wrong idea about the process being described by Self-Deification.

Self-Deification does **not** mean becoming some sort of omnipotent, all-powerful ruler, hurling thunderbolts about the place. Not even close. It means three distinct things, not one of which is popular with dilettantes:

- acceptance of total responsibility for yourself, your decisions and your actions, together with their consequences.
- assumption of total sovereignty over your own being and your world (i.e. the environment with which you surround yourself and which you use to reflect you).
- consciousness of your own highest principles and values, being true to your ideals of Beauty and Valour.

The above is the kind of Divine consciousness we are talking about. The problem is that people see the word 'God' and immediately respond to programming, picturing themselves sitting on clouds, being wrathful and omnipotent. Tough luck, you're still playing the incarnation game and you'll still need to join the rest of us pushing your trolley round the supermarket.

The quality that we are speaking of is that of **personal** Divinity, becoming the sovereign and absolute arbiter of your own life, defining your own purpose and goals, living by the code that you create for yourself. The small print reads, "Superpowers not included".

The other aspect that we need to address is the feeling of awe we experience when we realise the scope and span of the Universe, which can make us feel so small in comparison, paling any notion of personal Divinity.

Don't forget that consciousness is the interface between the Void and the Cosmos, the shaping factor, and the factor which affords meaning and purpose. And although yours may only be a tiny spark of the Flame, this consciousness is nonetheless yours, the most precious thing in all Creation. No matter how vast and wondrous and awe-inspiring and beautiful and frightening the immensity of the Universe may be, it only possesses these qualities because you are there to perceive them. Whatever there is of majesty, of wonder, of beauty, of awe – these things are created within your mind. Without you to give them meaning, they are as nothing.

It remains to be reminded that Divinity does not mean ascending to some 'higher plane' and ruling from a distance. It requires immersion. The Universe is the means that has been created for the expression and manifestation of consciousness. It is not a prison to be escaped, as the slave religions would have it. It is the means of our Self-knowledge and Self-Becoming. It is the mirror that we hold up to ourselves. Living within this world is the **purpose** and the **goal**, the best possible place to be, with so many possibilities open for us. Here and now is our Heaven and our Hell, Self-wrought and beautiful beyond imagining. If you're looking for some kind of 'divine plan', “us is it”, right here and right now. Ignore it at your peril.

## The World Tree

In almost all magical schools, the Cosmos is likened to a tree. The most famous example is the Tree of Life of the Qabalah. The most useful and well-balanced model is the Norse Yggdrasil. The Celts also viewed the Cosmos as a tree, with the Otherworld Plains up in the branches and the Lands of the Underworld deep down among the roots, with the ogham paths – themselves attributed to trees – running between them. Shamanic cultures invariably envisage a world tree also, as discussed in Mircea Eliade's classic on the subject, *Shamanism.* So the model is all-pervasive and it is a very good one. But the World-Tree is a much more complex, complete and multi-dimensional model than has often been fully appreciated. A true Vision of the World-Tree is one of the hallmarks of the Sixth Head of the Apophis curriculum.

We may ask the question, "If time as such does not exist in the Void, why does it exist in the Universe?" But perhaps it doesn't. Perhaps time is nothing more than an illusion created by the way in which we perceive Reality.

Let's consider the World Tree not merely as a model of the mythic worlds and spheres of influence pertaining to a given magical tradition, nor as a psychological model of the Initiate's inner being, but as a model of a complex space-time event.

Yes, an event. One single event, which encapsulates all of space-time. The trunk of the tree is where your perception currently resides. Looking back to the roots, you see all of the choices and paths which led you to this place. Looking up to the branches, you see all of the myriad possibilities that are yet before you.

But here's the crux of it. Those roots and those branches are part of the tree **now**. They aren't past and future at all, they exist in all their completeness **right now**. The only distinction is the way in which you perceive and interpret them, in accordance with your illusion of time.

Imagine that every division of every branch and every twig is an alternative choice. This is something similar to the 'many worlds' theory of quantum mechanics, which suggests that every time someone makes a choice, all possible choices actually happen and the universe divides into several divergent courses. But we remain aware only of the divergence that our consciousness is actually **in**. The same is true of the past: every root and every division is another alternative route to the 'present'. And what of the present? The only reason our 'present' perspective appears to be a solid trunk is because we are only aware of the route we are currently following, not of the multitude that have diverged from it.

This gives us a model in which the entire Universe – past, present and future as we understand them – actually exists contemporaneously in its entirety, with every possible choice and divergence present in its complete structure. There is no time in the Universe, because the Universe is complete in its every possible manifestation as a single, timeless whole. It never changes, it simply is what it is.

The only thing that changes is consciousness. We incarnate within the world, then we follow our choices through it, moving from one branch to another as our decisions dictate. But **all** branches exist. We only see the ones that we travel along and cannot see the alternatives because we are within the Universe, not seeing it from without (or at least not until we have become Initiate enough to Open the Eye in the Void).

If this model of the Universe as World-Tree has merit, then there is no time in the Cosmos, just as there is no time in the Void: the entire kit and caboodle exists all-at-once. The Universe is complete and unchanging. The only thing that changes is **consciousness**, as the incarnated ego navigates its path through the Tree, depending upon the choices it makes. This would fit the purpose of the Universe exactly: it is an arena in which consciousness is free to explore and express itself. Consciousness is the **only thing** that experiences change and transformation, which is possible because of its restricted perspective when immersed in the world. This, the *Xeper* of the individual Self, is the whole purpose of manifestation, enjoying life in the playground.

Mention of play brings us back once again to our remarkably apposite metaphor of the Cosmos as a video game. Because when you buy a video game on a disc, or download it as a software package, the entirety of that game universe is contained in the code that you install on your computer or games console. Everything that can possibly happen in the game is already coded and exists within it. The game contains no 'time factor' as such. The only occasion when time becomes a factor in a video game is when you, the player, enter that virtual world and begin playing, making your choices and exploring. But all of the choices you make dictate responses which have already been coded; the impression of an unfolding, developing in-game world is pure illusion, albeit an immersive and engrossing one that sucks you right in. The Cosmos is even such, just on a grander scale. The only aspect of the game that actually changes are the parts of it that unfold within your own mind, the story of your character within the world and the way in which he / she develops in response to your in-game actions.

As in 'real life', most players are content to play the game at this level, enjoying the experience and immersion. Some will seek out and discover the little inconsistencies, bugs and quirks in the game's programming, which they may exploit without technically 'cheating' and exiting the game world as it currently stands; this is a similar practice to Lesser Magic. Still others will use their knowledge from 'Outside' (Opening the Eye in the Void) to rewrite sections of code, introducing 'mods' to the program, which may change it in small or large ways, enhancing and expanding it to suit their wishes. This is a similar practice to Greater Magic.

## Are There Other Universes?

Once an Initiate has got his / her head around the notion of Reality as a whole being composed of the Creative Void, in which the Universe is a deliberately crafted and balanced island of relative stability, the question will inevitably arise: "Could there be other Universes?"

Theoretically, there's no reason why not. Perhaps the Void is like an infinite ocean, with an infinite number of Universes bobbing around in it like bubbles? That could be the case. But we don't know, and I'm going to stick my neck out and say that at our present initiatory level, we **can't** know, nor do we need to know. The question is one of those which springs up and immediately absorbs armchair occultists, who love to debate such things back and forth. But we cannot possibly know, and moreover, the question has absolutely no relevance.

As we have already mentioned, the Universe in which we now find ourselves is so immeasurably vast that the idea that we might possibly outgrow its lessons and experiences and potential any time soon is absurd, so laughably arrogant and ignorant that the notion really needs slapping down and put in its place.

I've only brought this question up in this book because

I knew it would be asked and I wanted the opportunity to state that any true Initiate needs to stop wondering about irrelevant theoretical bullshit like this, stuff that can simply not be known and wouldn't make the slightest difference if it could, and instead get back to the Work. There's a whole Universe of joy and experience to be had right here, and **that** is our Task.

The kind of people you'll find discussing things like this back and forth are bullshitters pure and simple. On the one hand, they're the worst kind of people for a true magician to mingle with, as they'll distract you and annoy with their trivial, inconsequential chatter all the time. On the other hand, they can – just occasionally – be the best kind of people to associate with in the short term, as a clever Lesser Magician can lead them on all manner of merry dances to his / her own advantage. And yes, they do deserve it!

## WHY BE A MAGICIAN?

Some of you will be scratching your head and wondering why this is even a question. But it's actually a very valid one. Unlike nearly all religions, Draconian Magic is perfectly happy with the idea that most people aren't followers of its own creed. We really like the fact that the world is filled with all manner of ideas (though of course we'd prefer if some of them weren't so psychotic and insecure that they try to insist that everyone else adhered to the tenets of their beliefs). It is perfectly possible to live a very full and happy life without ever entertaining the slightest idea of magic. And that is a wonderful thing. It's not going to cost anyone their 'immortal soul' to do so, there's no blame or harm or guilt in doing so. In many ways, that's precisely what consciousness wants, just to live a life, with eyes wide and a sense of wonder. Nothing could be more precious. A life well lived is its own reward indeed.

Those who become magicians are those who've probably undergone the incarnation process quite a few times previously and have become old hands at it, able to peer behind the curtain at the stage settings of the world. They become magicians in order to enhance their understanding and experience of life, and so that they can continue to learn and evolve – carrying more through with them from one life to the next through increased Self-integration – which is the whole aim and ultimate purpose of manifestation: the Becoming of the Self.

This is a process which occurs of its own accord as the Self accretes enough *Xeper* to actualise it. It cannot be forced or learned by those not ready for it, because they won't grasp its principles, as evidenced by the frothing, ranting internet 'mages' who lack the insight or self-knowledge of a duck's arse. This is why every occult Mystery can be clearly stated in plain words and yet misunderstood and completely glossed over by those not ready for it. Every Initiate is familiar with the heated internet debates between insistent know-it-alls who have quite evidently not glimpsed even the first principles of the subjects they are pontificating upon so hilariously. This is a sad fact of the situation when the occult is fashionable and spouting crap is easy[21].

The **only** reason for becoming a magician is because you have Become a magician, in the sense that your own Understanding and Self-transformations have brought you to that place.

21 As a footnote for those who knew me as a young, inclusive Magister Templi a couple of decades ago, yes, I have become much more scathing, cynical and dismissive of fools as the years have rolled by – much to my credit!

## WILL EVERYONE ONE DAY BE ENLIGHTENED?

This question is a consequence of the same kind of wrong thinking that is discussed in the first paragraph of the previous chapter. It erroneously assumes that there is somehow something 'wrong' with living and enjoying a simple, ordinary life, with all of its everyday joys and woes. The question is riddled with the same old bullshit that our society has programmed us with for generations, ever since the putrescent desert religions spawned by fuckwit Abraham took a grip: namely the supposition that life is worthless and meaningless, that we are a miserable species in need of some kind of salvation.

Ain't the case!

It also buys into the insecurities fostered by most religions and belief systems, whereby if we believe something, then we feel that everyone else must feel and believe the same way, otherwise it somehow invalidates us. News to you, people: if you are a magician, aspiring to be one of those Gods we mentioned earlier, you need to grow up and learn to be your own sovereign. You need the validation of no one, nor is anyone else's Becoming any responsibility of yours. It's not your place to decree how they live their lives, and you definitely don't want or need others to shape how you live yours. These are ingrained bad habits, wrong thinking that must be shed.

So will everyone one day be enlightened? Who knows? Who cares? In the meantime, so long as they're alive and conscious, their consciousness is experiencing and learning, gradually coming to know and understand more about its own being, though the good times and the bad, and that's pretty much what life is for.

Everyone who possesses consciousness, sentience, a sense of Self, is **already** enlightened in the most important sense possible: they have realised that they exist, that they live, that they are individual. Some will embrace this, some will fear it, it will inspire some and subdue others. But all will deal with the realisation in their own way. Because that's precisely what being an individual consciousness, a Self, is all about, and it's nobody else's business to interfere in that process unless comparing comradely notes **by invitation**.

Just to open your eyes and face the day with a sense of wonder: that is enlightenment enough. Anything else is down to the individual.

Does any of this mean that animals too have selves and can experience enlightenment? Very probably, if their consciousness evolves sufficiently to spark into Self-awareness. This is a fact that no pet owner will doubt. But that consciousness is for them to shape and exercise and enjoy, not for us to dictate.

## What Ifs?

To close this series of reflective essays, it seems appropriate to close with a couple of 'what if?' scenarios that have often been thrown my way.

The first is a favourite of evangelical Christians, who will wring their hands in despair at the fate of my soul and plead with me, "But what if, Michael? What if I'm right and God exists and you haven't accepted Jesus Christ as your Lord and Saviour? What then, when you stand before God on the Day of Judgement?"

The answer is simple: I'd stand there proud and spit in the bastard's eye. Because if their God did exist and was anything like the vicious, sadistic, psychopathic monster portrayed in their Bible, there is no way I would bow my knee to that twisted abhorrence! I would stand proud, and the evil fucker would have to make sure to pack me off to Hell pretty quickly, before I had chance to boot him in his almighty balls. Such a horrifying, savage entity warrants no worship, not out of fear and definitely not out of love. So you can stick your 'what if?' up your arse and toot tunes with it!

The second 'what if?' is a much more reasonable one and merits proper consideration. This is when I'm speaking with a rational materialist, who says to me, "You're so involved with this magic stuff. Doesn't it worry you that it's getting in the way of living your life? What if there's nothing in it, if it's all fantasy and self-delusion? What if matter is all that we are, and there's nothing after death? Aren't you afraid that you may be wasting your life with this stuff?"

There are three answers to this question. The first one is flippant, but true, and is simply that if it's all self-delusion and there is nothing beyond death, well, I won't know about it in order to be disappointed in that case, will I?

The second answer is basically contained in the *solve* and *coagula* parts of this book. It will be self-evident that I assert absolutely that magic works, and works reliably. Once the magical 'knack' is learned, it is something that can be depended upon to deliver. But it is also apparent that I would argue that nearly all magical success comes through natural channels and can be explained by processes activated within the psyche, which empower the magician to achieve things he / she may ordinarily have deemed extraordinary. Although there are exceptions to this rule, most successful magic is of this type, so even in a completely mechanistic Universe, I would still claim that the practice of magic is a tremendous tool and advantage for those who can learn how to use and apply it effectively, as described in the chapter 'Runes For Sceptics'.

Of course, as this book proceeds beyond that point, most especially into this latter section, speculating upon such matters as the Void and rebirth, we are once again entering into the territory of things which are not immediately or definitely verifiable. They are the best possible answers I can come up with, based upon the model of Reality I have experientially found to be the least problematic, the most comprehensive and the most satisfying. But these things remain open to challenge. I – and you, as my reader – must always remain aware that these things are theories and working hypotheses which seem to fit the facts. If they ever fail to fit the facts, there must be some flaw with them, which will need to be identified and addressed. But at no time is it likely that these things will be demonstrably proven. So I have to freely admit that some of the further flung ideas of the philosophy, psychology and cosmology offered in this book may be incorrect. But since I'm open to new ideas and new information, since I have an open mind and am working with my current best possible model, that's perfectly okay. It's important to never let these things crystallise into a dogma. The purpose of a model of Reality is to help you understand the Real, not to obscure it.

The third answer is specifically addressed to the **study** of magic, its characters and its history, its language and its symbolism. Perhaps our sceptical friend may admit the usefulness of certain magical practices, accepting the presentation in the 'Runes For Sceptics' chapter, but will find fault with the time spent meditating, poring over old books, memorising tables of correspondences, and just the whole dark and spooky aesthetic of magic. “Surely,” he may suggest, “it is a waste of your time to indulge in all these things, to the detriment of other pursuits?” My answer to this one is simply that everything we choose to do is of necessity done to the detriment of those things that we choose not to do. Because we simply can't choose to do everything. And my response in favour of the study of magic is that even if his worldview is correct and there is no tangible benefit from it, I find it interesting, fun and fascinating, and that is reason enough to do anything!

I hope this book has succeeded in annoying you and causing you to question your ideas, because that means that your ideas will become better and stronger in consequence. And may your magic always be interesting, fun and fascinating, as mine is for me!

# Other Draconian Magic Titles by Michael Kelly

## APOPHIS

A practical handbook of Draconian Left-Hand Path Initiation. The Primordial Serpent lurks in the deepest, darkest roots of human consciousness. Each of its seven heads embodies a power which may be awakened within the psyche.

'Apophis' outlines the transformative process whereby the human Initiate becomes something much more than human. It provides the weapons necessary to win the war of consciousness against conformity. It openly teaches the means of immortalising the Self.

# Ægishjálmur

### The Book of Dragon Runes

*Ægishjálmur* takes the curriculum of Draconian Magic – powered by the Dragon energies that lie in the deepest parts of the human psyche – and applies it within the context of the runic tradition of Northern Europe.

The myth of Sigurd and the Dragon Fafnir is used as a heroic role model for the Initiation of the reader, who is guided on a journey of discovery which unlocks the hidden powers of the body and mind, opening consciousness of higher dimensions and timeless states of being.

The student is empowered by the polarised energies of the three great Dragons of the North: Fafnir, the guardian of riches; Jormungandr, the Midgard Serpent who establishes the boundaries of the world; Nidhogg, the primal Dragon of Chaos, who transcends life and death.

# Dragonscales

*Dragonscales* is a collection of essays and articles which supplement the Initiatory curricula presented in *Apophis* and *Ægishjálmur*. The articles may be read alone or together with the other two books in the series.

These essays explore some of the Draconian themes in greater depth than was possible within the scope of the basic curriculum, providing new avenues and techniques for students to explore. In particular, this book's contents shed much more light upon the higher 'Heads' in the Draconian initiatory curriculum, providing much food for thought for the more advanced student.

With expanded lore, practice and philosophy across a broad scope of subjects, this book will prove invaluable to all who Seek After the Draconian Mysteries.

# Draconian Consciousness

## The Book of Divine Madness

*Draconian Consciousness* is the fourth book in Michael Kelly's Draconian series, and is intended for advanced students.

This is pre-eminently a book of 'doing', a practical manual of Work to be performed by the Initiate. It is a challenging and demanding curriculum which gives no quarter and pitilessly turns many cherished ideas and notions on their heads.

This book was penned from the heart of the Void. It is deliberately full of the contradictions and about-faces that characterise the Abyss where time and space no longer exist. Where most occult books fail to deliver, there is REAL power here, use it at your own risk.

The time has come for Apep, the Ancient Dragon, to swallow the Sun. Let the consciousness of the Dragon permeate your mind. You will never be the same again. NOTHING will ever be the same again.

# Words of Power

*Words of Power* is the latest in Michael Kelly's series of Draconian titles. Its purpose is to reveal the Mysteries of the spoken and written word, and how the precise use of words is essential to magic.

The book is divided into three sections:

In the first section, historical traditions of magic are studied with specific reference to the ways in which they use Words and Names of power. The Graeco-Egyptian magical papyri; Qabalism; the grimoire traditions; runes; ogham; Enochian; Satanism: all are examined closely and their techniques dissected. This demonstrates how the entirety of magical practice is founded upon words and their correct use.

In the second section, attention is turned to the use of our own contemporary language as a tool to influence and persuade others, utilising the skills of Lesser Magic. The secrets of persuasion are laid bare, with a full discussion of how to choose the right words to convey the precise meanings and emotions which will persuade others to do what you want, whether you are talking to an individual, addressing a crowd, or using the written word.

The third section looks at the Draconian characters created and used by The Apophis Club, demonstrating a method of drawing forth your own personal sound keys by accessing the qualities associated with various letters in your own subconscious. These words and letters are then explored further through three levels of numerological analysis.

The reader of this book can expect to come away with not only increased knowledge of the power of applied language, but the skills and techniques to choose the right words to create the changes he or she most desires. For magic is the fulfilment of desires, and this book will show you how to fulfil yours.

# Grimoire of the Sevenfold Serpent

*The Grimoire of the Sevenfold Serpent* is a small handbook of purely practical, results-oriented magic based upon the Seven Heads of the primordial Dragon and the teachings of The Apophis Club.

In this handy booklet, the sorcerer will find techniques for evoking the essence of each of the Seven Heads and applying their powers to achieve worldly success. There are also instructions for invoking your personal Dæmon, an important consideration in boosting the power of your magic.

Here you will find a useful shortcut to harness powerful energies for those who are new on the Path, and who wish a foretaste of the unearthly consciousness which is their Draconian heritage.

# Gods and Monsters

*Gods and Monsters* is a collection of five profound and challenging writings by some of the foremost members of The Apophis Club. These essays seek to address the nature and essence of entities such as Gods, Dæmons and Spirits from both practical and philosophical standpoints, offering up new insights and tools to Initiates of the Draconian current:

- *Vampyric Alchemy* by Steve Dee and Lucien von Wolfe. This study examines the archetypes of the Lycanthrope and the Vampyre, and the ways in which they may be awakened and used in the process of Self-transformation.

- *At The Left Hand of the Goddess* by Matt Anon and Durga Mahavidya. An in-depth study of Indian Tantric practice (the **original** Left-Hand Path), with particular emphasis upon the role of taboo-breaking female Divinities within this current.

- *The Dragon in Antiquity* by Joyful Hydra. A detailed study of the initiatory importance of the Dragon in the roots of mythic traditions, with particular emphasis upon the Indo-Iranian mythology. Contains the necessary keys to apply such mythology in practice, as well as understanding it within its proper context.

- *Haunters of the Dark* by Michael Kelly. A study of ghosts, hauntings and the spirits of the dead. Focuses upon the possible causes of hauntings and culminates in a necromantic experiment to determine the fate of the soul after death.

- *Remanifestations in Rheged* by Jez Green. A personal account which demonstrates how Initiates can go about connecting with the mythology and spirit of the landscape that surrounds them, providing themselves with powerful foundations to stand upon. Witty, informative and profoundly practical.

MICHAEL KELLY

# Runes of Mann

*Runes of Mann* is a study of the runes used by the Viking settlers on the Isle of Man approximately 1,000 years ago.

The first part of the book describes the exact set of runes used by the Manx runemasters, a variant of the set of sixteen runes known as the Younger Futhark.

In its second section, the book gives detailed descriptions, illustrations and photographs of many of the runestones that have survived on the Island since the Viking Age. Stones bearing the Celtic ogham characters are also described and pictured.

The third section of the book seeks to recreate methods whereby those interested in using the Manx runes for divination or magic may put them into practice today.

An important book, both historically and practically.

# The Sevenfold Mystery

The Enochian system of magic, received by Dr John Dee and his clairvoyant colleague Edward Kelly in the $16^{th}$ Century, has fascinated magicians and occultists ever since the Hermetic Order of the Golden Dawn adapted its mysterious Tablets and language to their use.

Enochian magic was the force that established the dominion of the British Empire in Elizabethan England. It was used by the Golden Dawn and Aleister Crowley to invoke incredible visions of the Magical Universe, and has been in use by occultists ever since, with frequent tweaking and adaptation.

This new book on Enochian magic aligns the system to the Draconian methodology and curriculum of the Apophis Club, marrying the parts of the system to the Seven Heads of the primordial Dragon and creating a powerful engine for Left-Hand Path Initiation in the process.

The book is divided into five sections:

- A clear, precise summary of the core parts of the system
- A discussion of the Work of Dee and Kelly, and how the system was first derived
- An overview of other individuals and groups who have Worked with Enochian
- The bulk of the book comprises the detailed grimoire of Apophis Club Enochian Initiation, a series of ritual Workings, meditations and challenges which will lead the successful practitioner to the pinnacle of Self and into the heart of the Void
- A discussion of the apocryphal *Ordines Descendens*: Satanic Enochian magic

The author says: "There is tremendous power to be found in this book and the Work it contains and it is my ardent hope that it will be as useful and transformative to others as it has been to me. I make no apologies for sacred cows slaughtered along the way, nor for necessary innovations. This is a book for progressive magicians, not Elizabethan purists. And I really do believe – for reasons that will become apparent – that John Dee would approve of the progress that has been made and that time has not stood still."

MICHAEL KELLY

CPSIA information can be obtained
at www.ICGtesting.com
Printed in the USA
LVHW052246300423
745713LV00014B/1385

9 781533 302007